poemmemoirstory

Number Four / 2004

PMS is a journal of women's poetry, memoir, and short fiction published once a year in the spring. Subscriptions are $7 per year; sample copies are $5 with appropriate postage. Unsolicited manuscripts of up to five poems *or* fifteen pages of prose are welcome during our reading period (September through November), but must be accompanied by a stamped, self-addressed envelope for consideration. Manuscripts received at other times of the year will be returned unread. For submission guidelines, please see our Web page at www.pms-journal.org, or send an SASE to the address below. All rights revert to the author upon publication. Reprints are permitted with appropriate acknowledgment. Address all correspondence to:

The University of Alabama at Birmingham
Department of English
HB 217, 900 South 13th Street
1530 3rd Avenue South
Birmingham, AL 35294-1260

friends

staff

editor
Linda Frost

assistant editors
Delores Carlito
Margaret Harrill
Sue Kim
Heather Martin

administrative assistant
Stephanie Smith

layout & design
Russell Helms
Meg Walburn

cover design
Michael J. Alfano

cover photo
Lynn Ledbetter

contents

poem**memoir**story

poemmemoir**story**

Welcome once again to another round of the most exhilarating *PMS* you're likely to have! At least it's pleased *Best American Poetry* editors Yusef Komunyakaa and Lyn Hejinian, both of whom selected poems from *PMS* for inclusion in *Best American Poetry 2003* (Ruth Stone's "Lines" from *PMS 2*) and *Best American Poetry 2004* (Carly Sachs's "the story" from *PMS 3*). As always, our pages are home to the words of women across the country, from here in Birmingham to San Francisco to Findlay, Ohio—and beyond. This issue's featured memoir, written by a woman who has experienced something of historic and national significance who would not necessarily describe herself as a "writer," comes from Mary Eila Smothers, a member of the Alabama Army National Guard serving with the U.S. Army 214th MP Company in Baghdad. Her description of what it's like "Here In Iraq" raises many of the questions we have all been dealing with the last few years: "how long will all this go on?" for instance, as well as "how will it change who we are?"

Aside from the current events into which Mary Eila gives us an intimate look, *PMS 4* offers a revealing cross-section of the preoccupations and expectations of women writing today. For Nicaraguan-born poet Maria Vargas, that means finding a good dream; a difficult task, given that her dreamer can only come up with a "measly little" one "the size of a small cabbage." There are poems about the dangers of fashion—"Eddie Bauer" and "Abercrombie&Fitch" both make an appearance here—as well as the ever-present problem of body image as captured in Denise Duhamel's loving lament about her "Lip Lines." There is, as always, a sweep of work about loss—the loss of love, one's own life, one's child, one's faith, one's chance to belong, one's worth. But in the writing there is reclamation, even when there seems to be none. As esteemed poet, dramatist, and activist Sonia Sanchez puts it in her burning "He/She:"

No delicate
strands of hair
here. Just wild
sweet strands
rising in
magnificent
flight.

Such flight abounds in *PMS 4*, including unexpected flights of fancy. For some reason, this issue drew three separate stories about people exhibited as, or discovering themselves to be freaks; it's certainly a theme, one combining feelings of alienation with the power that accompanies the telling of one's tale—or "Tail." One of these stories belongs to Ada Long, a woman to whom we at *PMS* are in great debt. She has been emotionally and financially supportive of us since the beginning, and she let us use her own house—the Honors House at the University of Alabama at Birmingham, that is—for our Publication Party last year. The work she has done has already touched many, but we're not-so-secretly pleased we can extend her clairvoyance even a bit further via our pages. In honor of her in this year of her retirement, we dedicate *PMS 4* to Ada.

And there are plenty of other folks to thank. *PMS 4* has been made possible in large part by funding received from the Alabama State Council on the Arts and the National Endowment for the Arts. We remain grateful for the financial gifts of UAB's School of Arts and Humanities and UAB's Department of English, as well as our blessed patrons and all our lovely Friends of the UAB Creative Writing Program. Individually, the support of folks like Bert Brouwer, Marilyn Kurata, Bob Collins, and Dan Butcher have continued to make our existence possible and pleasant; collectively, it is only with the help, guidance, and very hard work of my staff that this thing happens. Stephanie Smith helped out on the administrative end while Lynn Ledbetter and Michael Alfano gave us yet another stunning face. My assistant editors, Delores, Margaret, Sue, and Heather, are just the most fabulous helpmeets for which any editor could beg. They all read like troopers and took care of countless, thankless, crucial details. I love them. And I love the folks at Menasha Ridge Press too, the crew who handled our production for this issue. I am particularly partial to a certain Acquisitions Editor who works there and with whom I share an address. He and our lively young ones, Lucy and Cora, keep me holding on.

Finally, thanks to you, our readers, *PMS* is a dream once again realized. Dream it well!

Linda Frost
editor

poemmemoirstory

Heather Burmeister

CROW.

an ache in the crow's nest
eyes shouting: take that!
they are sword bearing eyes
they metamorphose into an aunt
saying: we are all in this together.
pivoting brain. running machine.
the light a sharp sting at the crow's feet.
I am a crow clicking across the linoleum
clutching beads, anything shiny.
I peck at a glass of water
and ignore the phone.

PMS

Tammara Lindsay

ABERCROMBIE&FITCH (since 1892) 1. That magnanimous bronzed blonde in a blue-eyed gaze is the signature; a perfect equilateral triangle of flesh holds his head together. How can I find meaning in all that glow and indifference? Ex. I love him (in the false sense). 2. I see gift bags floating his image over sidewalks like divine intervention. I feel him feeling me, the weight of an invisible dumbbell as I walk past his tremendous display case. Ex. I hate him some days when my pupils dilate toward his image. 3. Abercrombie, your music is like a bag full of broken glass. You contain multitudes; you're a religious sphere for the saved and fashionable. It hurts to pass through light like yours: the blaze, the holy t-shirts, pious jeans, That Man.

EDDIE BAUER, where do you come from? You are everywhere squeezing a lemon into your drink. You have tipped your hat to some woman's breasts (nice tactic), and kissed the concrete because you're alive in America, a diappointment to your namesake. You're a Gatsby in disguise, an immaculate scarf pulled over large blue eyes. The word on the street is these threads make a better person, that these signature turtlenecks transcend markers of class. Sharp. Everybody buys because "they're worth it." You have an eye for foolish.

Elaine Equi

JOHN COLTRANE'S CENTRAL PARK WEST

Now this is the music
I imagine playing
if I were having an affair
with myself as a married man.

   It's the music that would
always remind me
I always have me
in a special way
even if we aren't actually wed.

Elaine Equi

THE LONG FOREVER

The face is just more
storage space.

Who keeps insisting
it's not a hostile makeover?

The hand clutches
a sandwich-map

as tone on tone turns
in its soundtrack.

Brick after empty brick,
once was once…

this voice is dubbed.

Marianna Hofer

THIS MORNING COULD BE THE NEW WORLD

One day, as every good self
revelation story starts,
you wake up, the curtains
billow about the bed,
the neighbor slams
the truck hood shut after
again tricking it
to start, and you feel
very close to convincing
yourself things will stop
shifting or shattering like
a well trained chimera,
a badly mishandled mirror.
You know, of course, that
isn't near the truth, but
like the windchime on
the curtain rod above
your bed, it sounds
good, full of promises.

You tell yourself stories
most days just before
you leave the house, careful
they don't all have happy
endings. The tiny movies
unreel at stoplights, while
the waitress refills
the tea, the wind plays at
the hem of a long skirt.

As a girl you lived with
a man you ceased to think of
as a lover. One chore there
was to weed the lily bed
which took hours, dirt
and sweat pricked at

your skin. Once you napped
afterwards in the grass, felt
a hurried small breeze,
heard a persistent whir,
opened your eyes to
a hummingbird close enough
to see every tiny ruby
and emerald feather at
its neck. You know then
you would move
back to the city.

You wait on the curb. A land
scaper's truck comes around
the corner close enough
to smell the peat
and gravel. The boy
you wish for sits in
the passenger seat, arm
braced in the open window,
doesn't see you. You watch
the truck blend into
rush hour traffic, then
cross with the light.

Tonight you sit out
in the rainy air, listen
to the sirens, wonder
what's gone awry, who, what,
needs to be set right,
gathered up, calmed down
by people trained to stop
the situation before it goes
all to hell. Months before,
just as you turned into
a kiss from a stranger,
you wanted to run away.
Here now, the rain rushes to
the low spots, gathers
and runs into the drains.

WITHOUT DREAMS

The last real one she remembered was the dream about an actor rehearsing "The Autobiography of an Egg." That was 1968. She was jealous of people who dreamt of ambergris, aviculture, ABSCAM, almonds, Australia, the Age of Aquarius, the Ace of Hearts. Her cousin Beulah told her about nights full of cracked wheat and Jerusalem artichokes.

The Asian continent was a great longing, but above all, she wanted to dream about lizards, dry figs, the Cocoas plate, the Amazon! She wouldn't have minded (such was her desperation) J. Edgar Hoover, preachers, mosquitoes, or even Hitler's big toe (something!) in the blank screen behind her eyelids.

She went to a dream specialist, Dr. Sriniv LeJuan Rodriguez Tang-von Hottenberg Lefkowitz, the only child of two well-known New York psychiatrists who, in spite of his peculiar physiognomy and a problem with continuous blinking, came to her with impressive credentials: he had slept for eleven months and achieved three and a half dreams per day. Doctor Rodriguez Tang-von Hottenberg Lefkowitz recommended Siberian ginseng, ashwaganda, chlorella, and gotu-kola: all she managed was two minutes of microscopes, pesticides, and rabbis.

She tried magnet therapy: a magnet in her ear for exactly forty-nine seconds before bed (one second longer would bring plaid wall paper, yodelers, and rhymed poetry about Jesus). The results were medium-sized icicles and square buttons and a single image of an artificial leg.

She visited Ayurvedic, Hindu, Voodoo, and Chinese doctors who promised Rabat, apricots, umbrellas, and the Mediterranean. The Mongolian acupuncturist explained the wonders of eucalyptus and pennyroyal which would surely produce dreams of oriental villages and rain forests and would also keep her free of moths and fleas.

One of the magic potions made her sleep for twenty-seven days. She dreamt of Kafka and a Turkish one-eyed woman with a talent for metaphors. She expected tangos and purple. She received gray and silent. She desired luminescent lullabies and sonorous serenades. Her efforts produced opaque odes and less-than-radiant radishes. For the rest of her life, she dreamt one dream per night: one measly little dream the size of a small cabbage.

PMS

MAYBE SIBELIUS

This morning there's a bit of Sibelius lodged
in my brain, a motif, repetitive, longing.
When I put words to it, they're the Beatles'
—"I've got to get you into my life." Last night,
wild thunderstorms, lightning for hours after
the storm passed over. I dream you and I
are making love in a room next door to grief,
that bleak presence aphrodisiac. This after a day
on which you irritate me, I bore you. At cross-
purposes, we gesture concessions, fail to signal
anything more than a vague wave at some mirage
of compromise. I think you're obsessed with
our son, you that I'm obsessed with the garden.
I know what I'm not talking about, I only guess
what you're not. In the dream we are dancing
while making love, to improbable music, maybe
Sibelius. What is it I must get into my life?
Long lapses, rests in the music. My heart turns
over when I catch myself thinking if you died
I'd become a hermit. I already know what that
dream signals: on the other side of the wall from
bliss there is anguish. I can't sleep nights though
I'm not obsessing about anything. The story is a
ronde: A loves B who yearns for C who's mad
about A. A is the question, B the answer, C is
the demurrer. Yes, I'm obsessed with the garden.
I want to spend all day on my hands and knees,
smelling the soil. I want another life to listen to
opera, one to read Dante, one for Proust. One
in which to become a hermit. I'm jealous when
our son answers your emails, not mine. The rain
is a sudden burst, deluge. You are what I have
to get into my life. You are what I have. What
if, hurtling through these storms, we forget to
touch, to make the gesture that will heal us?

Sandra Kohler

SOMEONE ELSE'S LOVE POEMS

He is writing the poems already, less than
a year after her death, that I imagine she imagined
his writing: poems of her death, of his looking
back at her death without her, living without her.
There is a rich oval of black ice on the edge of
the deck, dark gleaming jewel. How did it come
to freeze just that way, to be what the flood left
after torrential rain, sudden precipitous freeze?
Two mourning doves fly overhead, side by side;
one, landing, skitters as its feet hit that patch
of ice, waddles off, clumsy and iridescent.

The intense pleasure of being first to rise, make
the coffee, walk around the house which is silent,
filled with presence. Like Didi and Gogo: alone
and together, together alone, alone together.
In my dream, my husband is discussing stocks,
investments, the necessity of not risking capital
with the banker handling our money, while I
gather soiled clothes for the final wash which will
take care of every unlaundered item, kneeling
and scurrying, harvesting dirty socks from
my husband's suitcase, disrupting its order.

What is faithfulness? What is faithlessness?
What is there to be faithful to but the possibility
of faith? The sun is faithful to earth, but that is our
illusion. The sky is faithful to nothing but itself,
the birds don't track its loyalties. Sparrows swoop
in and out of the sky's disguises. The Korean
dogwood is sheathed in ice, strange apparition:
where has this garment come from? A long
finger of ice, a white bier, floats down the creek,
solemn, processional. Mid-January, on the day
of the rains, the temperature rises, then drops

forty degrees, the river rises, thickened by ice,
the creek overflows all bounds. That day a robin
roosts in the scraggy mulberry, astonishing,
breast glimmering pale orange against the snow.
Pattern, order, the rhythm of seasons seems
an invention we cling to. Freak weather insists
it is only freakish. We don't predict, we live it.
I imagine living past your death, imagine writing
the poems of loving you when you are no longer
in the world. I imagine being struck silent,
buried with so much unspoken.

Four Variations on Loss

I.
All those pairs of glasses lost on the ocean floor;
how do people find their way, nearly blind?

No chance to stop the slow descent without
a lightning grab, or some amazing sleight-
of-hand. Instead, they zig and spiral down,
their sightless lenses coruscate, the glare
of loss hits sharp and sure. It's not the thing
itself you'll miss; replacements can be
quickly found and seem perhaps more flattering
at first, the newness pleases you. What's lost
beyond your fingertips, beyond your ways
of holding on are words like *mine*, like *ours*—
they're gone before you have the slightest chance
to gasp, to wish them back, to say next time
you'll be more circumspect, more vigilant
of treasures held that slip away when backs
are turned. Before you know you want them still,
you watch them spiral down.

II.
Lost things prey on your mind; you can't help but picture them,
perhaps happier, somewhere else.

Imagine somewhere in nameless depths
mermaids adorning themselves with rings
they happened upon in watery caves,
weaving found charms into their hair
or pinning baubles to their scales,
an iridescent competition.
Fish blink without recognition.
They snap at glittering prizes
drifting past in a slow descent;
they've mistaken them for sustenance,
for life.

III.
A garden should be left where it's planted.

Leave loosestrife borrowed from the neighbor's woods
to purple the hill below the gate; beneath the kitchen window
foxglove and yellow tansy must also stay:
they were chosen for this house, this life.

IV.
Don't try to count the things you've lost; something important,
something that might have mattered, may be forgotten.

So you draw back your empty hand;
no plumes of bubbles stream to the surface.
The only air sucked through gritted teeth
is all above the glassgreen plane
separating *above* from *below,*
held from *lost.* What's felt
is a monotonous unspooling,
like a kite string playing out slowly
sending the paper diamond rising,
rising and burning bright before it falls,
drifting like ash to get lost
in the deep green trees.

But we are speaking of how things
work loose, how they fall
into profound absence,
not simply out of reach
but unreachable. Lost things sink
without a murmur or a sigh of regret.
Tears are wasted; there's no way to tell
where they end, where they may have started.

Still, light pushes deep
into the complicated dark,
refracting on paired lenses now blind,
or a single golden hoop
forever without its mate.
And what of other treasures lost,
beloved things that drifted beyond your grasp
while you clutched at empty air,
your mouth a startled O

Karen Maceira

MARCIA, DYING OF CANCER, SPEAKS TO A CURBSTONE

I begin to tell the world goodbye.
I choose you, first, little lip.
You restrain the eager path
with its promises of ease.
And you keep from that path
the wild-eyed houses
with their strange noise:
caterwaul and huzza.
How many times I left that wilderness
just to feel you firm against my bottom!
I watched pebbles caught in pitch,
and I admired your slow hoard—
wrappers skittering, hopeless
bits of gravel, dull pennies.
Most of all, I
have loved your composure,
articulate
edge of intensity.

Carla Panciera

THEY COULD BE MOONS

Recently, and by someone who meant it as a compliment,
I have been told that I hold the tether to Planet Earth.
At the end of the strings in my hand are my closest friends,
as liable to float away as a bouquet of balloons
when the carnival man forgets himself and applauds.

They could be moons, my friends, or ruling planets.
They could gather themselves in chatty constellations,
inspire mythology about stars who share truly funny jokes.
Unimpeded, they might view sunsets, meteors,
the Super Bowl, or weddings of their first loves.

Except that I hold them, my good friends would star
in weather reports, be sighted like birds or objects
that give us some hope of life out there despite the flat,
thick dark. They would be heavenly bodies turning
cartwheels through the astronomer's scope.

Weight problems, cowlicks, the hassle of finding
comfortable shoes, of keeping dust off furniture—
these things and more would be past for them, if only
I would let go where I stand, letting my sneakers fill with mud,
my assistant, the breeze, as unpredictable as sanity.

Kathleen Roxby

WITHOUT NO SHOES

I walked the hills without no shoes
(never did have no shoes)
I rode the trees in the wind
And smelled coal every day of my life

Blackeyed Susans blessed by heart
High-reached water blessed my tongue
And the wide sky taught me to dream

I walked the hills without no shoes
Into woods only the deer knew
I rode the trees in the wind
And smelled coal every day of my life
While the wide sky taught me to dream

In the quiet of hidden meadows
Blackeyed Susans broke my heart
High-reached water awoke a lasting thirst
For I smelled coal every day of my life

I walked the hills without no shoes
(never did have no shoes)
But I rode the trees in the wind
And the wide sky taught me to dream

Trish Steinley Davis

FLOATER

Through sun-dappled water
my two-year-old child sinks
into the deep end. *What fate
has pulled her down?* I remember:
wet diapers are heavy, baby fat floats.
Quickly I must make a choice.

But the movie slows; I choose
to stare into a faceted aquamarine
inside which a baby smiles and floats.
Once, a South Asian child silently sank
from his parents' boat. I remember
they never reached for him: fatalists.

Not thwarting divine will, that's fate.
Kicking off shoes: an unconscious choice
in an eyeblink. Who can tap or recall
the sacred position? Sun-dappled water
tickles her ears, cradles my child sinking
or—depending on perspective—floating.

Through blue-heavy water she floats,
slowly downward. Think: what is your fate?
Would it harm her if I dove, would we sink?
Did she baby-toddle off or boldly choose
to reach for the faceted aquamarine?
The first time she floated free, I remember

she bubbled up from deep inside me. *Memory,
mine:* she meets my loving gaze. *Hello, floater.*
Eight seasons later, beside sun-dappled water,
I think: we must select among alternate fates.
No longer part of me, what will *she* choose?
My two-year-old child, into the deep end, sinks.

I kneel on rough decking, heart sinking
with her into softly lapping azure. *Remember*
not to fear. If we choose well, our wills, choices,
reactions will be in sync. She seems to float
up as I reach down—a meeting of fates,
a taut cord (flaw?) in the faceted aquamarine.

Sinking fingers into her shirt: marvel of flotation.
Memorable, yes, plucking child, gratitude, Fate's
choice from the deep, sun-dappled water.

Lynne Thompson

Quicksand

May held on for a long time but that's over.
Even in the backwash, there are no answers
and you're a fool if you think so. It's all
global warming and sinkholes now. Yet,
it's ok, you say; you're a trumpet lamp
with a handmade shade; you're a thousand
costumes with matching shoes. And love?
You're its darling dumpling potsticker!

It's sad really. Watching you run around,
lost, with no papers. You will never return
to the home you once knew. Oh, maybe
some dog walker will hire you to tame fleas.
But look at what you're holding in your lap—
it's October and you don't even know it.

Lynne Thompson

Marriage, A Fugue

Which naked body is yours? You were salt at breakfast but by cocktails, your asters were in bloom. The length of your spine may bow for a cello but still I would know that you are betrayal. I'm lost as a girl but hallowed be my ova, hallowed be my tongue, hallowed be the soles of my feet but halleluiah, you're sure a stranger. Call me when the cycle's over.

Patti White

THE OWL AND THE PUSSYCAT

Oh you should have seen them.

He rowed right up to her daddy's door
come to claim his bride on the appointed day.
Robert's not one to let the river stand between
him and Miss Hilda Johnston, and she was ready

looking out the window of the second floor parlor,
her kin, the canary, all of them peering out, laughing
a little, but impressed, and a little scared too.

The good lord only knows where he found the money
to pick up a boat, and there's not a one of that group
can swim a lick, not Robert nor Hilda either, land-locked
every one of them. Also she's fat, and he's a clerk.

I mean, a farmer, now, can row a boat with some strength
at least, even if he's no sailor, but still, this boy's got guts
and imagination, and before long he's got her in the boat
and they're headed for the Presbyterian Church, to the parson.

At this point they're out of my sight, but the church itself
had two feet of water, so they didn't go slogging up the aisle,
but went up the steps to the little house, and inside
just as pretty as you please.

They'd planned to go up to Pittsburgh for the honeymoon
(we don't go in much for Florida or Niagara here),
but the road was closed, so they came out man and wife
and he took to rowing her around the town, showing her off,

cruising along pointing out the sights she knows so well
but that seem so different now, and not just because
everything's all wet and muddy and strange;

and, I know this because they went right past me,
his voice takes on a lilt, and all of a sudden he's singing
to her, and she sits there, a brand-new missus, and listens
with her head tilted to one side, as serene as the queen of cats,
not a thought of trouble in her head, afloat on a sea of cream.

Patti White

ISHMAEL

The hardest thing for me was the animals.
I've spent all my life with livestock. When I was a kid
my pa gave me a calf to raise and it was a treasure to me,
it seemed like biblical riches, greater than rubies. Chickens,
pigs, a couple of goats, mules for work, horses for the wagon,
all of them precious, the life blood, to breed and husband,
which means to care for, to foster, and I take that as sacred,
a Christian duty. So watching them drown, finding them
bloated and rotting in the ditches, snagged on barbed wire,
that was hard.

       When the water rose so fast, the first thing
was to save the people. I know that. But it hurts my heart
to think how confused and bewildered the cattle were, adrift,
swimming hopelessly in the currents of the river, wondering,
freezing cold, trying to find footing on a bit of wood. Pigs
perhaps smart enough to realize the dangers around them,
the snakes, the floating logs, whirlpools; and the horses,
good god, those beautiful necks straining to keep the heads
above water, and finally going down.

       I didn't use to dream,
but now every night I see the animals swept into the flood,
hundreds of them drowning one by one, and the last,
a yearling calf, swimming in circles around me, just
that one left, his eyes locked on mine, and then the river
just takes him away, downstream, and the water
is empty, and it's just me, and I have to carry them,
all those deaths, a burden on me forever.

PMS

Janet McCann

THE WOMAN WHO COLLECTS NOAH'S ARKS

Has them in every room of her house,
wall hangings, statues, paintings, quilts and blankets,
ark lampshades, mobiles, Christmas tree ornaments,
t-shirts, sweaters, necklaces, books,
comics, a creamer, a sugar bowl, candles, napkins,
tea-towels and tea-tray, nightgown, pillow, lamp.
Animals two-by-two in plaster, wood,
fabric, oil paint, copper, glass, plastic, paper,
tinfoil, leather, mother-of-pearl, styrofoam,
clay, steel, rubber, wax, soap.
Why I cannot ask, though I would like
to know, the answer has to be simply
because. Because at night when she lies
with her husband in bed, the house rocks out
into the bay, the one that cuts in here to the flatlands
at the center of Texas. Because the whole wood structure
drifts off, out under the stars, beyond the last
lights, the two of them pitching and rolling
as it all heads seaward. Because they hear
trumpets and bellows from the farther rooms.
Because the sky blackens, but morning finds them always
safe on the raindrenched land,
bird on the windowsill.

Janet McCann

SOMNIA

you sleep and the dog sleeps,
   sometimes you think
you have slept up all the sleep,

and are tossing in dreams
    snatching at rags of blanket,
        your hips scraping at rocks.

nowhere is deep enough to stay there
    the dream shabby and fragile
your fingers poke through and touch the cold

the patter on the roof humdrum as fingers
    tapping on the dream-bar
      where your order never comes

though you wait for it in half-light
  and the other grainy-faced patrons
all seem to be served

the mattress hard and narrow
      no one even in dream
calling out your name

as you rise and fall in sleep,
      the dog with you,
billows and hills of sleep.

Halsted Mencotti Bernard

WITH TALONS

Driving into my narrowed gut, your eyes
say nothing, read everything out of me.
I find your whisper at my neck
overwhelming. My breath, a gust out of me.

Say nothing. Read everything. Out of me
you take what you want; your lips are always
overwhelming my breath. A gust out of me
and I reach for you with talons.

You take what you want. Your lips are always
painful to watch when not on my body.
And I reach for you with talons,
with everything, but I come up empty.

Painful to watch when not on my body,
driving into my narrowed gut, your eyes
with everything, but I come up empty.
I find your whisper at my neck.

Karla Clark

BECAUSE OF THE NOISE THE BIRDS MAKE quarreling or

so joyous almost garbled   inarticulate with praise

because the light in the cup is amber   then like almonds

then like milk

Whatever happens changes   in the space between event and mind

Once we thought love dangerous   not to have

exactly but to say   that we were something less or naming

it would then be stripped away   like onion skin

birch bark

Amazing to sit over breakfast this way   our faces turned toward

each other   in the hedge some wind-scruffed cardinals

bend their red heads toward the sea   little geckos click

and turn suddenly green   on the patient trunks of the palms

Karla Clark

LONG MARRIAGE POEM

Late March. The light months beginning; in countries such as ours
                         calves are born, people start to laugh.
Laughter, because the violent awakening of cherry
trees is frightening.

Frightening and miraculous, the color pink along a bough.
Laughter because air is suddenly full of the sexual scent of
orange.

I remember sensations like this from the early years,
                        fear and laughter,
simply because your back was beautiful,

freckles, muscles, whirls of hair, sharp wing-bones under your
skin.

Downtown: the plaza underneath frothing trees,
people drinking coffee, balancing their bikes against low walls,
and by the market, a young woman suddenly cartwheels,
                        perhaps her boyfriend sent first irises.

Crucial
these sensations, like
a sweet-water well, dug deep,

quiescent until needed.

Oboe music in the distance. You lifted your face to the mountains
as far as I remember, changed in no detail, that moment
as we this morning almost
joyful, almost ready to remember
how to hurl our bodies through the fulcrum of the acrobatic turn;
              upside down and laughing in this piercing green.

Wendy L. Burk

LYRIC

Are you seeing things again?
Undoubtedly. Because
there is a place for everything
in the dark, whose open unicorn
settles down to lick me, softly…. Who
will take issue with the issue
of the night? Whose spiny legs,
emerging from an alley, spider
longer and longer, till the light
blinks out—now it's a tree,
holding itself and sobbing.

PMS

Carly Sachs

FROM THE STEAM SEQUENCE

<pre>
                              in
              the   tea
the   woman
                        bathing
in   a   blue   bathroom
                          steam

                                    rising
                from   the woman
is burning
                          the dim light
       in   the   room
                    the moon
</pre>

Carly Sachs

FROM THE STEAM SEQUENCE

steam   rolling   off

                          her body

the skin   peeling   back

the music
            thinning

                      to air

Lip Lines

With the war and plastics and carcinogenics, with my tenure file and computer
virus and high cholesterol, it's crazy to worry about the wrinkles over my lip,
those lines that my lipstick has started to seek into, red rays around my mouth,
red caterpillar legs. John said a few years ago, "Don't worry, Denise, you'll
never get those. Only smokers get those wrinkles over their lips from sucking
in," and I believed him, hoped those lines would stay on my forehead, around
my eyes, but now they have come to roost, over my lip, even though I never had
a cigarette in my life. I wonder if the lines came because I sucked through so
many straws hoping not to mess my lipstick. I'd heard straws also kept diet coke
from staining your teeth. Yellow teeth, another thing I worried about. But now
the lines have come, encroaching on my vermilion border, the almost invisible
line just outside the colored part of the lips. I always took my vermilion border
for granted, though it would always be a soft carefree no man's land. And then
when I went to get my eyebrows waxed, a few days ago, the technician said,
"Will that be all?" and on the way home I kept staring at my downy mustache in
the rearview mirror, the mustache which draws even more attention to the
crinkles around my lips. I stare at my lip lines after I brush my teeth, pay morbid
attention during Botox commercials. I put extra Oil of Olay around my lips at
night. I research anti-aging creams on the web. I worry about colon cancer, it's
true, and car accidents on I 95. I worry about not having enough money to pay
the mortgage or buy groceries, which you'd think would put my lip lines into
perspective. Oh little lip lines, tiny haiku, lines of 5/7/5 resting on their sides.
What would the Buddhists advise? *Make friends with your lines.* Easy for them to
say, especially the old wise monks with their sweet young skin, living in the
right climate for decades, talking to no one.

Denise Duhamel

SELF-PORTRAIT IN RHYMING SLANG

I'm artsy-fartsy, ac/dc, always slumped in front of the
boob tube. I'm the bee's knees. I'm a bag with a sag. I'm a
culture vulture with a cheat sheet, a chopper-copper, a
double trouble dizzy Lizzy. I'm date bait, a dead-head, an
eager beaver who likes things even-Steven. I'm a
fat cat fag hag playing footsie wootsie with a fancy-nancy
glad lad. We're a gruesome twosome going to a function at Tuxedo Junction. I'm a
hootchie kootchie who's paid a handsome ransom.
I'm alive 'cause I dig the
jive. I've been known to smoke a
killer diller kick stick with a
lame-brain legal-eagle lane from Spokane. I'm loose as a goose. I have a
mop-chop. My best friends are twins, Mike and Ike. Though I'm full of mojo, I'm a
no-go nitwit. A nitty gritty no-show. I'm a
okey-dokey ooly drolly
piggy-wiggy. I'm a peek freak who spies on my passion ration. I'm a teen
queen with a
rootin'-tootin' rabbit habit. I'm rum-dum,
sake-happy, skirty-flirty. I'm a square from Delaware, a silly billy who likes a good
thriller-diller. I'm a tootsie-wootsie who talks
ubble-gubble. I'm a
virgin-shmirgin with VD. I'm a
wheeler-dealer keeping up with white flight on my walkie-talkie. I'm an
ex-hexed Tex-Mex
yuk-yuk of a yo-yo.
Zodiac-schmodiac! You'll recognize me by my zoot snoot.

PMS

Eileen Murphy

CHEATING

I was long on the crossword puzzle
    then on two pillows
        in bed on Sunday
           afternoon
when in my in my July sleep
    vibration & gurgle
        like someone pulled the plug
          on a giant bath
           tub
must be thunder & I am on my side &then thunder
    legs are bent
        & mild eyes goodnighting
          home
from treadmill/yoga
    with my sister has lost one hundred pounds
        & stretching hurts no matter how sister how I'm
careful to
        baby
the shoulder where the January operation
    still smolders & the operation & I ask myself which drug
        on today's menu sacks me sleepy so & then
          thunder

Zan Gay

Letters to a Foundling Home, 1892

1.

      Dear Sister,
he drank my wine, fingered my hair,
left the next day, so I feel
to put my little one with you for a time.
Not anywhere there's a good lady to have us both
while I polish her brass doorknobs, fry her onions.

I bring my baby knowing you will sing to her under elms,
wash her feet.
She is not yet christened with a saint's name.
Give her one, ancient and sweet with the sound of wind.

I curl up in a doorway severed from my child,
twig from branch.
My solace that if I am spared
and lead an honest life,
I will return strong and brown-eyed,
carry us two 'cross river.

2.

Dear Sister, no words come
this paper blank   I stare at table
pencil   my hand ready to write
a few lines. Thanksgiving night
between the hours of eight and nine
I remember the snow in the lane
stripped birches and the child I held
without a slip of paper to tell you
her name   Janie Janie Janie born
October 5 between the hours
of three and four   a piece of canton
flannel tied around her head like a
little blue and white cloud around

and red socks on her feet.
I am numb with cold
I left her in your good hands.
I am her mother   have no sweater
to send   so sorry to have nothing.
I keep my dress clean, rinse my hair
with lemon. I can read.
Pray for me, there will come a day
when I'll bring my daughter pearls.

Mary Kaiser

SUPPERTIME

She lifts her arms high, high
and spins, lifts and spins,
and spins in circles
round her grandmother's yard,
round the big oak tree and the Adirondack chairs,
their sloping seats low
to the ground, their generous arms open,
waiting, but she can't stop now,
round the bed where
black-eyed-susan petals spin
round their velvet centers,
round the green mirror
of the fish pond, round
the compost heap baking and steaming
in the afternoon sun, out to the corners
where Easter eggs nestled and
rubber balls disappeared,

until her grandmother comes
down the walk, untying her apron,
and catches her and, laughing,
holds her tight, brushing
the damp hair off her hot cheek,
holding her so close she can
see how the white rick-rack
dances along the scalloped
collar at her grandmother's
deep-caved throat
and how the soft lines
of her grandmother's cheeks curve
down to complete the perfect
oval of her face, and she
knows it is time to slow
down, leave the shadows
lengthening in the grass,
and follow her grandmother inside.

Irene Latham

PARALYZED

She spends her days looking out the window,
her body a cloud her mind waves away.

The sun shines on, oblivious,
paints the grass in waves, the trees

in pale watercolor strips that fade
from brown to green. Gone

are the ridges and knots, the broken
branches, the individual veins.

She strains to remember the last time
she climbed a tree, tries to recall

the bite of bark on her palms,
the nip and tuck on thighs. She wants

to swim in memory, but her mind
sits like a pond in the distance,

without shimmer or reflection, a flat
unspent quarter of silver light.

At night she dreams of falling. Not
about the point of impact or the moment

after. Just what came before: the rope
turning venomous, striking flesh from each finger.

The wind forcing her eyelids closed,
steely rock-face peeling them back,

leaving a hole through which the rest of her body
did not have enough time to escape.

She dreams of snowy ibises settling to the ground,
their gentle descent marked by eerie grace.

She dreams of lovers she has yet to know,
of bottomless kisses she can't run from,

of arms reaching to catch her.

Mendi Lewis Obadike

WILLOW, WEEP

> *Whisper to the wind and say that love has sinned.*
> —Ann Ronnell

Her cruelest tongue, turned meek. Her saddest lips. Her bite.
Belly swole, but slimming. Stair step father looking,
his reproach. Why does he hate the father, lacking?
Have you seen him? Whose cheekbones in her baby bright?

Wind, blow away from here this hush. Tree, make a moan,
and say what you know without seeing. Whisper this.
Bend and tell it. Her belly. Meek, her saddest lips.
His reproach, his randy smirk. Baby. Whose cheekbone?

Her baby. His approach. Looking, lacking. Father.
Her tongue turned. His looking. Blow 'way from here. Day, break
this hush. Do not see. Shine light behind her eye. Weight.
What can you know without hearing? Does he hate? Her

Tongue turned meek. His randy smirk. What is the lesson
of this hush? Day, break. Dig this from the ground. Shine right.
Do not see a smile. Hear what is dragging the night.
Willow, weep. Whisper what you know. And you, listen.

45

Mendi Lewis Obadike

LEARNING TO LISTEN

You say
I look like
a Buddhist monk.

At first
I don't take that to mean
you want me.

Sonia Sanchez

He/She

She. ferocious
with flesh.
He. amputated
at birth.
She adored him
in spite of
her blood
ricocheting
off her knees
floors. Kitchen.
She cried until
the morning descended
on her. She
stooped into his
arms where he
grabbed her
between kisses
pretending
he didn't do it
didn't mean to do it
wouldn't do it again…
No debutante
eyes here.
No delicate
strands of hair
here. Just wild
sweet strands
rising in
magnificent
flight.
No. him. sweetening
up the air. here.
Just an urban-city
musical about
family

fading into
autopsies.
Maybe she thought
after she rubbed
the welts. She
thought maybe this pain
he painted on her body
was his Art
his celebration
of self.
Maybe he thought
after he had come
inside her three times
and he was too soft
to receive further adoration.
maybe he went out
to find music where
maybe the agony of being
Black. Latino. White. Asian.
would not quarantine him.
She remembered that day
which was like no other
throbbing like youth
but older than young
high-stepping assassins.
She noticed the hairs
growing out of his nostrils
measured the spit capped between
his teeth.
saw his eyes shifting
in purgatory.

He had traveled all
night and morning in
community creases of anger.
He replayed the night
jokes about yo mama his mama
other oiled bitches
perfumed in paradise.
Don't get me wrong
he said, I love the
smell of cunts.

Catacombs of blood
and lies.
Imagine.
The shiver of death.
Imagine.
finally the absence
of pain escaping her skin.
Imagine.
Holding one eye
in her hand
only the TV
breathing news.
Imagine.
Her prayers landing
on the ceiling.
I am sorry he says I am
sorry he says I am sorry
he says forgive me he says
forgive me he says forgive me
he says he says he says
and he holds her close.
As she closes her one good eye
she discovers she is humming
blood clots
or is she running
head still on her shoulders
other eye in her closed hand.
She tastes the slow
arrival of God.
What presents does He bring?
What does He know?
About One woman.
One man.
Alone.
Faces.
Spellbound....

Lois Marie Harrod

YOKE

And what did I hope for when I hoped, immortality?
That gold coin passed from one hand to the next

then suddenly lost in a drawer, closet, chink, dropped
so that an earthquake later, volcano, hurricane,

it can rise to the surface where gold has no value
or small. When I was thirteen, I hoped fairy tales,

the fish on the table cleaves open, and lying there,
the endless life in its gut. I am a princess, I am a beggar.

When I was 15, I memorized "Thanatopsis"
while I was ironing my father's shirts

because my Latin teacher said everyone should know that hope
by heart: So live that when thy summons

comes, you will be starching your father's collars.
Didn't the old book say something like that?

It is always been my hope to cram more things
than possible into the possible, the collar first, the stays, the yoke,

the cuffs the sleeves, this is how it is done, first things first,
the bed, the lip, the mouth, the rising up, the lying down.

Naomi Levine

THE UNBRAVE

Failing focus
through myopic predisposition
and not daring
to foray into faulty erudition
I stick to simple senses' play
and feast myself, and say my say.

poem**memoir**story

Blood Meal

There is no playfulness as we approach the city.

Poverty is vivid, not a ball that children are being taught to throw at foreigners to see what comes back. There is desperation here from a sun that sears the flat, dry land and stagnant chocolate puddles. There is lawlessness here—enough for me to check my belongings for planted drugs or smuggled goods that someone in a uniform at the Moc Bai border may have stashed.

The closer we get to Phnom Penh, the more prevalent the begging becomes on the roadside. Children no more than ten years old cup their hands, slump their heads, bend at the waist and freeze in this position as the bus whisks by. They are emaciated and nearly naked. It is a sight that stirs even the locals in their seats.

The trance of travel sets in.

So many extremes flash by: deformed faces begging in the streets, a woman breastfeeding her baby in a crowded intersection, the smell of tar and manure, foods that stare, piles of garbage and rocks, the slumped back of a woman working alone in the rice fields, a small boy sucking his thumb and holding a dead chicken in his other hand, a man pissing on a tree, a family of five loaded on a motorcycle, women covering their noses and mouths, long fingernails on men, traffic signs that say !, boys throwing sludge balls over a volleyball net, people playing Ping-Pong, a young girl standing alone and sobbing hysterically.

Movement never stops. Traffic jams. Fits and starts.

I glance at the driver and the large hairy mole between his eyebrows—a third eye that dances and blinks in the reflection of a loose mirror vibrating from bumps and screeching stops. He looks like some cartoon character I cannot place. In the center of his window is a neon "Love" heart stuck to the glass with tape and suction cups. I watch the little balls of yarn that anchor the curtains until my eyes grow heavy.

We reach Phnom Penh by sundown.

So many of the cities I have seen so far as a traveler feel familiar. In Phnom Penh, however, I feel uneasy and out of place. This is a frontier city attempting to rebuild after being leveled by tragedies. Those who survive reveal awesome resilience. I feel foreign here.

Later that evening, Alex, a British traveler I met while crossing the border of Vietnam into Cambodia, spots me at a corner restaurant called The Capital—a hangout for foreigners, correspondents and English teachers. We sit down at a table where two women are talking about the journey north to Siem Reap and the Angkor temples.

Alex is a wild-eyed cross between a surfer and the familiar depictions of Jesus Christ. He speaks with intensity about everything. From afar you would think he was telling someone how to deactivate explosives or walk through fire. All he's really describing are the ASA issues of color slides versus color prints.

"Is Siem Reap safe?" Alex asks one of the women.

"Who knows, but why come to Cambodia if you can't see Angkor Wat?"

The other woman shrugs and drops a spoonful of sugar into her soda water. The bubbles climb over the brim onto the table.

"If you go by water it seems to be safe," she says.

Alex and I are trying to gather information. There is never a need to be subtle about such a thing. It is common for one traveler to tell another stories and offer hints for the road.

"You've just come from there?" he asks.

"Yeah."

"And?"

"And it's brilliant." She pulls her chair up to the table and begins to describe the different ways around the base town of Siem Reap and the arbitrary admission prices set by the police, different for each visitor.

The conversation slowly turns into English beer comparisons and talk of hash stashes throughout Phnom Penh. I'm feeling detached and groggy, so I leave to find some food from one of the street vendors. Eventually, I reach my guesthouse with a high-grade fever.

Something is wrong. As much as I try to ascribe my malaise to fatigue and PMS, it keeps getting worse. Something awful is taking over.

I collapse in my nook.

Fleas and dust-sized mites cover my mattress. I observe their patterns and notice their quick migration toward the heat of my body. I drape the mosquito net around my cot and climb onto the sunken mattress. Usually before drifting off, I recite foreign phrases in preparation for dealing with the marketplace. Instead, I oil my skin with DEET and plug every orifice, a nightly routine since Indonesia, 64 nights ago.

The room becomes a merry-go-round as the night grows older. My eyes are losing focus. Burning red with thick goo.

I'm hallucinating. I see myself sitting on a street trying to open a can by slamming it on the chipped curbside. A dark silhouette hangs over me. Small, chubby hands with sharp fingernails are gripping my throat. Something with rancid breath punches my stomach and yanks hair from my head, one strand at a time.

My eyes look up at the gray ceiling. I see faces from my past and our moley bus driver with pearls around his neck. I'm the sister and daughter, the childhood sweetheart, the runner, the dean and director, the lover, the graduate, the guest. Morphed faces cackle at me, penetrate me, chase me, feed me fresh fruits. I hear a high-pitched squeal accompanied by rich, pounding drums. I smell rotten chicken and mint leaves.

My joints and muscles feel as if they are outgrowing me, stretching beyond what my skin can handle. Someone pulls my eye from side to side on a string. The string is caught on a rusty nail. Pint by pint, blood fills my ears, which reach the point of popping.

I pass out.

By now, all internal clocks are off. For seconds or hours or days, I detect something yanking at my pillow. I hear crunching and smacking that sounds like my ears are being pierced.

The sensation seems to be changing. Blood is being drawn.

I scream and blindly drag my body into a sitting position. More weakling panic. I'm trapped in an industrial spider's web. I tear at the mosquito net until my feet are able to ground my puffy toes on the floor. Groping, I find the lightbulb hanging from the ceiling and tug its string switch.

A dim, flickering light illuminates teal walls with pink trim. It also frightens something into the corner. I notice a wide hole in my mattress and pillow, now in shreds. I'm overcome with adrenaline. Bending over is punishment, but I must know what lurks. I bend down and feel blood rush to my temples.

Rose

Under the cot I spot the glow of two orange eyes. A foot-long rat looks back at me, then turns away to frantically claw at the corner, trying to dig an escape route. It is less than three feet away. I gasp and freeze. Maybe if I don't move it won't either. For a moment, it sits perfectly still. I believe my "playing possum" plan to be working. Then, to my shock, the rat races toward my face.

My visage elongates and makes room for a quick, shrill yelp. A blood-curdler. I attempt full body lift-off at the sight of this bold attack. Instead, my head and shoulders smash into the bottom of the heavy cot frame. I turn and ready myself for a car crash. Wet fur brushes my elbow. I'm relieved, momentarily, though quite sure I've broken my back. I also feel as though my ears are falling off.

Claws are slip sliding on tile. I jump back up on the bed and scan the room. I'm waiting for a chance to blind the beast with my blanket. One toss, then I make a dash for the door.

"Let me out!" I pull at the locked door and jump up and down. The blanket is moving toward me. I fall into the hallway and nudge the boy sleeping on a floor mat next to the entrance.

"Some rat thing is in my room!" He doesn't understand. He's staring at my face, a look of horror in his eyes. I mimic a life-size rodent by making ears and fangs with my fingers and hunching around in a circle. The pain of being so coherent is excruciating. He follows me to the corner of my room and slowly looks under the blanket.

"Watch out! It's wild!"

The boy lifts his head quickly and looks toward the window facing the dump heap in the alleyway.

"Open," he says matter-of-factly.

I feel let down. "Yes."

"We close."

I wait for more, but there isn't any more. "I go to another room, yes? I'm sick."

He can tell. He disappears for a moment then returns with a large key. By now I'm doubled over. He fills my bag and leads me to a room away from the alley.

"You go in here," he says. "Okay for you?"

I nod yes until my head falls backwards. No food. No water. No clue what to call my disease. I lie down on the bed with one eye open, drooling over my cracked, chapped lips. My breathing grows unsteady.

Twenty hours later I awaken to my dehydration. I squat over the hole in the floor and pour cups of water from the dripping tap over my head. An odd, bubbly rash covers my trunk and legs. I must get food and potable water.

Back on the main street, I reach The Capital next door and spot Alex. He seems to recognize my malaise like the face of another traveler.

"It's breakbone fever, L.J. Dengue."

I recall my pre-departure visits with my doctor and how he warned me about mud puddles, dogs in the distance, anything with wings, soil and shrubbery. He described hideous symptoms in graphic detail.

"Peel it, boil it or heave it," he said with a needle in his hand. He was fascinated with the 20-month journey I was preparing for. Our sessions were designed to tame earth, wind, water and anything that went bump in the night. Shots for everything in triplicate.

But there is no pill or poking prevention for dengue fever. "The female takes frequent blood meals. This increases the chances of multiple infections by a single mosquito. You'll feel like you're dying, L.J., but you won't. Just ride it out."

Alex fumbles through his pouch, hands me two horse pills and says, "Try these. I picked them up in India."

I smile but say nothing. He has extended a hand but I sit, suspect of what might be as wonderful as simple generosity. My traveling is intended to give room to intuition and to try new ways of life. A little voice tells me to trust his advice but not his cure. It is the same little voice that tried to warn me about an Aussie grifter four months ago.

I stare at the brown pills, then say, "No thanks. I'll get some rest first."

"I'll check in on you tomorrow before I head for Siem Reap," Alex says.

"Who knows what the night might bring." I'm slurring my words. I wave goodbye and buy bottled water and bread down the dirt road. In the midst of all that concerns me about my condition, I know I will never see Alex again.

"You want the Killing Fields?" a cyclo driver asks as I walk by.

"Maybe later," I say and start to fall over into a rack of bicycles.

"Feel okay, Miss?" He begins to tuck in his beige dress shirt. I'm fading.

"Any trouble, you look for me." He points to the word "Dracula" on his baseball cap and flashes his teeth. "Friendly Dracula, no problems, Miss."

I'm fading fast.

"Where you go?"

A wave is approaching. His open collar is beginning to look like the mouth of a cave. I point like the Ghost of Christmas Past to the guesthouse not far down the road.

He takes my bundle of water and bread and says, "I help."

I cannot imagine how Dracula interprets me. He must answer questions for himself because I am unable to launch into my "I'm-a-Christian-Teacher-and-My-Husband-Is-Here-for-Work" speech. He knows I am traveling alone.

Being "only one" is strange to many Asians I meet. Most see me and define my freedom in their own terms. Some assume I am free in other terms. Men turn and follow me with their hand in their pocket, or bark and whistle as I pass by.

I become a game and a goal.

My professional years had their own brand of intrigue. There were clever propositions and antics of men working with me on the road. I've been harassed verbally and sexually, trapped in rooms, pinned against walls, even serenaded.

With each experience I watched my womanly ways get bruised and grow increasingly bashful. Scar tissue began to alter the impact of violation. And, as with most things in life, the level of each occurrence became relative in comparison to the others.

These days are no different. My intuition brings judgement calls about strangers to an edge. I roam, regardless, but respectful of tragic consequences that may wait for me around each bend.

But let's not be foolhardy. I button the top button of my blouse, let down the cuff on my slacks and repeatedly take a flesh inventory: arms, legs, neckline—all covered. My face and hair are free of the woman's cloth walls, for I know that dressing the part is respectful in many of these countries, but not sufficient. I'm still in places where no other female will be, at times I shouldn't be, and alone—a way that few men would tolerate from their women.

I tread in the man's world as I never have before. I walk without swinging my arms or rolling my hips, trying to keep my breasts from moving. I cannot be a woman at all on some levels. On others, that is all I am.

Crowds of men often gather as I ask for simple directions. Many reach out their hand for me to make direct contact. I used to think they were being friendly, until a man in Fiji masturbated in front of me after I shook his right hand. The challenge as a traveler is to continually remind myself that, occasionally, someone in these crowds is just being friendly.

A torrential rain casts a moody light within my room. Dracula lines up several cups and cans to catch water from the eaves. The sound of them filling drop by drop is surprisingly soothing.

I feel his eyes looking me over, slowly. He watches my face rolling on the thin pillow. My lips mouth words to a high school ski team that I'm now sure is in the room with us. He lowers his stare to my bare arms and neckline.

My blue eyes and blonde fur struck many that I met in earlier countries. Some tugged on my eyebrows. Some threw stones at me or ran into their huts screaming and crying. Some turned their chairs to watch me eat. Some opened their homes and hearts.

Dracula only looks.

My abdomen is showing. Pale, milky white. My navel is filling with sweat. Large rib cage. Small breasts. He is taking it all in. I don't feel at ease, but I don't feel in danger. I feel heavy and lonesome like an animal in a zoo.

Something wets my lips. Both eyes open to see Dracula, who is wetting my mouth with his finger. He presses a damp rag to my forehead, then blows on my face to cool the fever.

There is a lingering voice in my head that expects Dracula to be like other handsome locals who charm a woman for days until her guard falls and trust starts to take hold. Then, and only then, does the agenda rise to the surface. Maybe it's sex or sponsorship in some form. Maybe it's a drug poured into her tea to knock her out. Maybe it's a long-term loan or a purchase of moonstones at five times their value. Whatever it is, something is taken when least expected.

But my friend is a gentleman in a vast, complicated culture.

Night after night I cross my arms over my chest, fold both hands in prayer and assume the position of a cadaver in her coffin. Dracula checks in on me and brings me food and water. He sweeps up my clumsy spills and washes my face with his checkered kramas.

"You have been kind," I say.

"You are only one."

His brown eyes sparkle with his smile. This is the image of his face that I will remember for the rest of my life.

I would have pushed his help away if I'd had the strength, and I never would have known how trust between two strangers could heal so deeply. When I was in a position to be taken, in every way, this stranger became the rare combination of friend and family.

Five days later, at the entrance of my guesthouse I extend my hand and kiss Dracula on each cheek.

"Thanks, my friend," I say and hand him U.S. currency that I had stashed in my passport.

Dracula seems embarrassed for a moment. He drapes his kramas around my neck and wishes me a safe passage. Thanks to him, I have mended enough to travel north to Siem Reap. We wave goodbye and, like so many people I meet on the road, he goes his way.

I continue on mine, grateful that humanity can bloom in the dark.

Jeanie Thompson

To Mike Kusmahn, With Regards, Where Ever You May Be

These are fictionalized memories. The names of everyone, except myself and the disk jockey, Mike Kusmahn, have been changed. The names of the two high school sororities have not been changed. Any references to actual people in those sororities are purely coincidental.

The summer I was fourteen I learned about baseball and the fickleness of social clubs. I learned to what lengths some girls will go to be accepted by other girls whom they think are cute or popular or important. During that time, I considered myself only vaguely cute and certainly not popular or important. Still, because Adrianne Collier called me every day that summer, I became convinced that by wanting something badly enough, I might be able to achieve it.

Which is where you came in. You were my hero, my friend, my secret Romeo of the airwaves. I claimed you as mine personally and listened to other radio announcers with teenage disdain. Every night, from 6 p.m. till 2 a.m., you played top forty hits and took special requests. But your favorite part of the evening was when you talked about your baseball team, the St. Louis Cardinals. They weren't merely your favorite team, the way people in Alabama favor one or the other, Alabama or Auburn. They were your team.

The Cardinals, led by pitcher Bob Gibson, were headed for the play-offs, maybe the pennant race, possibly the World Series. The World Series: those interminable games played in the lingering heat of fall and something we in the 1960s Deep South only experienced vaguely through TV or radio.

Time barely moves in a small southern town in the summer. In 1964, I was fourteen and absorbed in myself, my hair, my body. I drove my mother crazy with my alternating lethargy and restlessness.

Your voice was one of the few things that could soothe me, that brought me any relief. You were soft-spoken and exotic.

Radio-polished, your voice calmed me during my fits of melancholy. In the middle of blinding hot afternoons, I flung myself across the chenille bedspread in my room, letting the coolness brush my skin, swooning to the sounds of last summer's hit "Surfer Girl" as you played it for the twentieth time that week. At least once a week I would screw up my courage and give you a call. I would blurt out my request quickly, holding my breath to hear the modulated voice I adored. Over the phone, you sounded the same, though slightly more relaxed. I savored that moment when you spoke—Mike Kusmahn from the radio—just to me.

Adrianne called me most mornings and asked me to go play tennis on the school grounds between our houses, or to ride our bikes to the shopping center where we'd walk around McCroy's and look at records. The Beatles were making it big in America and we liked to check out their latest 45s. After baking on the sidewalks a while, we'd slide into the red vinyl booths of The Cookery and drink cokes and eat eclairs. Adrianne talked about JUG Club and how I should "want in."

"I think you can get into JUG if you decide to want in," she would start.

Adrianne' sister, Janice, was a member of JUG, a high school sorority which took its acronym from the full name "Just Us Girls." It's hard to believe that anyone could ever have wanted to be a member of a club with a name like JUG, especially one for teenage girls, but it was considered a classy organization. People were socially pegged for the rest of their high school lives—that eternity—by their acceptance into, or snubbing by, JUG and its sister organization SUB DEB.

Like any secret society, JUG had its symbols. The members wore a necklace with a single brown charm with the letters "JUG" engraved on it in 14 karat gold. I'll never forget the sight of that little charm laying just below the hollow spot of Amy Lichtenstien's smooth, golden neck. But for would-be members like Adrianne and myself, the coveted article was the pledge bow. Made of brown and yellow one-inch grosgrain ribbon, this bow spoke worlds. It said, "I am accepted; I am on my way."

Unfortunately, the bow also said that its wearer would have to undergo a pretty dismal hazing. The pledges were rushed in late summer when an eight-week torture period began. Sweet young girls from good families thought up humiliating tasks for their new sisters to perform. (Anne Macy, whose older sister had been in JUG about ten years before our class, told me stories about JUG pledges being forced to pee in a bucket outside of the A&P Supermarket.)

The initiation included all sorts of tasks and obligations including bringing an elaborate lunch to one's "big sister" every day during the final "Hell Week" and doing other jobs like washing cars. Hell Week culminated on a Saturday with a humiliating walk across the Tennessee River Bridge to the boat harbor where the pledges were forced to eat all sorts of concoctions in front of half of the town's teenaged boys. After that, the bows were traded for the JUG charms and gold chains, ordered at Diamond Jewelers in the Decatur Shopping Center. Here many JUG sisters would later reserve their china, buy their baby gifts.

I spent a lot of time that summer listening to you on the radio in my bedroom. I couldn't yet drive a car but I could tune in the old German radio my father had gotten on a trade from some friend of his and listen to you all night. The radio had a wonderful tone and a green electric cat's eye that told me precisely when I was tuned into your signal.

On Wednesday nights, you took requests for hits from the past. I tried to think of records that no one else would ask for, but I kept coming back to songs from the previous summer, things like "Judy's Turn to Cry" by Leslie Gore or "One Fine Day" by the Chiffons. I wasn't really into oldies.

On these nights, I called early in the program to be sure my song would be played. One night, I decided to ask for a silly song from the previous summer because Adrianne had a crush on her swimming teacher.

I called the station number and waited, breathless, my hands clammy, for you to answer. I always hated myself for getting so nervous. I had had the same reaction when I was a little kid in the choir at church waiting outside the sanctuary before we sang at Easter.

"WKRD radio," you answered, cool as could be.

"Hi!" I gulped.

"Hi, yourself," you said, laughing your short disc-jockey laugh, friendly, easy-going. Why was I ever afraid of you?

"Could you play 'Please Don't Talk to the Lifeguard'?"

"You bet. Who's it for?"

"Jean and Adrianne—I mean, Adrianne and the lifeguard." I was always self-conscious about my name since it could be a boy's or a girl's. I imagined you would think of us as queer.

"I'll do my best, Jean," you said and quickly turned back to identify "The Little Old Lady from Pasadena," as it trailed off before you hung up.

You knew my name! But of course you would. I had called you almost every week for six months. And I almost always dedicated the song to myself.

Sometimes Adrianne and I watched her sister Janice get ready for her dates. Janice was sixteen and had a lot of boyfriends. She was very pretty, with wavy dark hair, brown eyes, and a little pointed nose that I figured must drive the boys crazy. She was sensible and funny, not a giggly girl, and that made her popular.

We liked to sit on Adrianne's twin bed and watch Janice sitting cross-legged in her underwear at her vanity as she rolled her hair and put on her makeup. Janice had a ritual that we both memorized, waiting for the day when we could put it into practice.

It was the same every time. First, rollers the size of orange juice cans in the hair, then a cigarette while the rollers set, then make-up, and finally the finished hair itself. Janice pulled out the rollers filled with wire brushes, shook out her brown curls, and brushed her hair out into a smooth pageboy. Sometimes she tied a thick pink or yellow ribbon around her head in a style I tried hopelessly to copy.

Adrianne always made it a point to see that I got to talk with Janice or her friends if they happened to be around, for this was an all-important part of being seen and letting them know that I "wanted in." JUG was never mentioned as something to be achieved. That was taboo. The club only came up in relation to something concrete—the summer formal, or maybe a car wash.

On the night that JUG's arch rival, SUB DEB, rushed, Adrianne was baby-sitting for her little brother. He was four and too young to bring to the tennis courts after dark where we typically hung out. I had walked over by myself. Several cars were parked along the curb and a few kids from junior high were playing pretty bad games of tennis. A couple of older girls were sitting on top of the baby swings, those little boxes painted in primary shades of red, green, orange, and blue. I saw the tips of the girls' cigarettes glowing and heard them laughing. I felt awkward as I always did when Adrianne wasn't there to show me how to talk to high school girls.

I didn't see anyone I knew anywhere else around the courts, but I hated to go home so early. It was barely dark and going home then would set a bad precedent with my mother. I wandered over to the baby swings and recognized Dorkus Hughes and Elizabeth Warren, Nick's sister; Nick was my little brother Chad's best friend.

"Hi," I said as I sat down on top of the blue baby swing next to Elizabeth. Once I had seen a fat girl try to sit in one of these swings and get stuck.

"Hello," said Elizabeth, taking a deep drag on her cigarette. I noticed that she was holding a can of Budweiser between her knees as she rocked back and forth on the red swing. "You're Chad's older sister, aren't you?" she asked, looking at me.

"Yeah," I said. "I know Nick. I love him. He's really cute." I felt like an idiot saying this about a boy three years younger than me, but the words fell out of my mouth anyway, and just squatted there like a toad.

"He sure is," Dorkus said in her throaty voice and rolled her eyes at Elizabeth. They both laughed.

I was aware that this was a socially important situation. These were older girls and they had power. I felt sort of panicked that Adrianne wasn't there to take the lead. But I was relieved by the fact that Elizabeth and Dorkus were SUB DEB members and therefore no direct threat to me.

I hit upon an excuse to extend the conversation. If I bummed a cigarette from them, I could stay. I knew it was dangerous. My mother or even Chad could walk up, but I took the risk. I didn't care if the Surgeon General had just announced that smoking was harmful to your health.

"Elizabeth, could I bum a cigarette? I forgot mine," I lied.

"Sure," she said, almost graciously. To my relief, she produced a lighter and flicked it open as I put the Marlboro to my lips. It was stronger than Adrianne's Kents, but I managed not to cough.

"Hey, it's 8:30!" said Dorkus. "We've got to get over to Susan's." She jumped out of the swing and it arced forward.

"Right," said Elizabeth. "See you—" She stopped. "What's your name?"

"Jeanie," I said, flicking my cigarette ash. I was feeling slightly dizzy from the tobacco.

"See you, Jeanie," said Elizabeth as she threw her beer can behind the clubhouse.

At the curb, Dorkus gunned the motor in her Cutlass. As Elizabeth climbed in, Dorkus hit the SUB DEB honk: three short blasts, three more short blasts, and a final honk that said in code: "S-U-B D-E-B BEST!" The car peeled away too fast down the suburban street.

Alone on the baby swing, I watched the blue Cutlass turn down Raineford Road toward Susan Griffin's house. I wanted to let the smoke-sick feeling settle before I walked home to watch TV and call Adrianne. Maybe the Cardinals would win and you would be happy. I could call and request "Last Kiss" right before I got in bed and listen for it until I fell asleep.

Later that evening, I lay in my room on the floor talking to Adrianne. I had stretched the phone cord as far as it would go under the door and propped my feet on the bed. I hoped this position would reduce what I was convinced was swelling in my legs and ankles. I wanted slim ankles like Adrianne's.

We were talking about our favorite topic—older boys— when Adrianne hissed, "Listen! Do you hear that?"

I thought maybe there was a burglar in her house. I strained to listen over the phone.

"What is it?" I said finally.

"Go outside and listen. I think they're over around Country Lane," said Adrianne as she slammed down the phone.

I rushed out of my room, through the living room where Chad was picking out "She Loves You" on the piano," and out the front door.

At first I didn't hear it. Then I heard a car horn sounding a familiar honk: three short blasts, quickly followed by three more short blasts, then a longer single note. Quickly there were more, a chorus of them, overlapping. S-U-B D-E-B BEST! I counted to be sure. Again: 1-2-3 1-2-3 1. That was why Dorkus and Elizabeth had suddenly been in a hurry. I could see them in the Cutlass with a cooler of beer in the back seat. Probably Amy Rankin and Sue Yates were with them, too. They would all be laughing, honking the horn, drinking beer, hanging their arms out the car window, cigarettes glowing.

The horns faded for a while and then they came back, closer this time, only a few blocks from my house. For a split second I thought, "Maybe they'll stop here. Maybe they've been wanting me all along and I didn't know it." In a second, I fantasized the entire scene.

The string of cars would come honking the signal of my initiation down my street—S-U-B D-E-B BEST! Doors would open in one car before it fully stopped in my drive, and two girls (I couldn't see their faces clearly in my fantasy) would race to my porch, ring the doorbell, and throw open the door. My mother would not be at home. I would be grabbed, blindfolded, and whisked out to the car where they would toss me with several other quivering, laughing, crying girls. We would be driven away, the giddy notion that we were "in" numbing us like morphine. When I was brought home later that night, I would wear a blue and white beanie, cherished by SUB DEB members above all other possessions. I would be a SUB DEB pledge, my fate secure.

But instead I stood alone in the dark front yard, barefoot in the St. Augustine grass. I listened to the horns as they blared deeper and deeper into the neighborhood where other girls waited, girls who would be plucked unaware from a date's car or from whatever other mundane summer activity they had unwittingly chosen for that night of nights.

I saw everything as through a filter of rehearsal. I didn't feel truly left out because this wasn't the club I wanted to be in. I didn't know anyone who wanted in SUB DEB. And Adrianne, my best friend, wanted in JUG.

I remembered Adrianne and ran back in to call her, but her line was busy for a long time.

I will always believe that my mother planned our family's vacation that summer based on some insider knowledge. We left for Florida in late July and drove down to Tampa to spend two weeks with my grandparents. We toured Busch Gardens, picnicked at the beach, and ate lots of fish. I wanted to get a tan, find something exotic to wear, and meet a good-looking lifeguard. What I got instead was a deep burn that peeled and a lot of stares from older guys as I paraded myself on the beach. I was bold enough to walk by them in my bathing suit, but too shy to start a conversation. For exotica, I found a couple of unusual shells.

The trip back to Alabama was long and hot. The air conditioner in our car broke down and my father cursed a lot in greasy filling stations where we tried to find parts. Chad and I played off and on, but I grew tired of the games we'd invented for the riding in the car years before. At the Alabama/Florida state line, we stopped for sacks of grapefruit and oranges. The high point of our two-day trip home was a little monkey, who could do tricks, tied to a tree by the fruit stand.

The night we got back into town, I called Adrianne. I wanted to give her the shell necklace I'd brought her and was dying to go to the tennis courts to see everyone I'd dreamed about for two weeks as I walked on the beach or suffered the family gatherings at my grandparents'. As I had wandered in the conservatory among the giant fig trees and rubber plants at Busch Gardens, I had entertained myself by imagining that Webb Michaels, a senior, would suddenly appear from behind the bank of philodendrons and express surprise at seeing me. Coincidentally he would be staying near my grandparents'. There would be a date at the local drive-in, a moon-lit stroll on the beach. We would become involved during our Florida summer romance and return home going steady.

Adrianne sounded happy to hear from me and said to meet her at the tennis courts around 8 p.m. I told her to bring the cigarettes because I hadn't had one in two weeks.

I left after supper, despite my mother's protests. "You're too tired," she had said. "You've been in the car for two days."

"And that's why I want some exercise!" I said, grabbing my tennis racket and slamming out the door.

I wanted to run down the alley, but I had spent a long time on my hair and didn't want to mess it up. I crunched down the gravel to the school playground and saw Adrianne, already there at the big swings, talking with a couple of tenth-grade boys I had seen around but never met.

"Hi!" I said, putting down my racket. One of the boys said, "See ya, A." and they both walked off.

"Hey, Jeanie, I missed you!" beamed Adrianne. As she turned toward me, I saw the strip of brown and yellow ribbon clipped to the right side of her head.

I stood there in the late summer sunset, knowing in a flash that it was all over. I took the swing next to Adrianne, thinking, *on vacation with my family*. The wild thought that JUG might still rush me late flitted through my head as I kicked off in the swing.

"Did you have a good time?" asked my friend.

"No-o-o-o," I sang out. I felt numb. I pushed the swing toward the pink and orange streaked sky. "It was boring. I thought I would die."

"Any cute boys in Tampa?" Adrianne asked.

"Loads!" I said, swinging higher now. I wanted to cry, to be at home in my room, to hide my bare head.

After a few minutes, I came down to an abrupt stop in the swing on the darkening playground. Adrianne stood up, produced a pack of Kents from her shorts' pocket and said, "C'mon, Jeanie, I brought the cigarettes."

I followed her to the backside of the clubhouse, away from the street, and we lit our cigarettes. I wanted to say something, but couldn't. It was dark now and I could sense that Adrianne was happy, proud of her bow, and every question I could think of (when? who else? what was it like?) all pointed to my exclusion.

I hadn't thought of Adrianne in—and me, out—of JUG. It had been a plot hatched by us both, including us both.

Finally, after some silence, Adrianne said, "Janice said you almost made it." Her cigarette glowed red in the dark as she held it in her fingers in the style we had practiced: first and second fingers straight out, cigarette crossing the T.

"Really?"

"Yeah." Then she added, "Maybe you can get in next year."

I knew that she was offering me hope and that I should take it for sustenance. But I felt like I had passed through a wall, thick and tangible and chilling as the one I'd seen in a Saturday morning horror movie, a wall through which there was no coming back. The bow was in Adrianne's hair, not mine.

When I returned home that night, my mother was in the kitchen, putting away the picnic supplies from our trip. I knew she would quiz me about who was hanging around the tennis courts. Sure enough, when I walked in the door, she began. "Who was up at the tennis courts? Did you have someone to play a game with?"

I didn't answer her or say anything for a moment. I just walked over and picked up a couple of grapefruit from the bowl on the counter. I stood there, balancing them in my hands. It was hard to tell my mother when something was hurting me, and it was no secret that she despised high school sororities. I think in that moment I realized why she hated them, why she had never encouraged my "wanting in," why we'd rarely even discussed it.

"JUG rushed Adrianne," I said, still balancing the fragrant fruit. I raised one to my nose, sniffed it, and added, "while we were gone."

Mother stopped cleaning out the picnic basket and looked at me.

"You can still be friends with her," she said. She paused and then added, "You know you don't need JUG."

I knew she was right and resented it bitterly. I didn't want to admit that I didn't need what I'd banked on.

"Yeah," I said, putting the grapefruit back in the bowl. Crossing through the kitchen to the hall, I said it again, "Yeah, sure."

You would probably have encouraged me to forget it, to sit with my mom and talk. If there'd been a ballpark in our town, you might've suggested that my dad take me there. And he probably would have.

But that summer, as it turned out, you had other things on your mind. You weren't on the radio that night, or the next, and when I called in to ask about you, the new announcer said that Mike Kusmahn had gone back to St. Louis, had taken a job at a station there, a big break. The new announcer sounded like he was talking with his jaws clenched. His voice was too deep and he didn't sound real. Not cool and soft-spoken, not soothing and Midwestern. Just a redneck in disguise.

I hope you're out there on the radio now. I think a woman might still find comfort in your voice, might still listen to you when her world shakes and teeters, when a wall closes behind her, when she's still trying to hope. If you are, please play some songs from 1964, think of girls who dreamed they were going to be beautiful, that romance was possible in exotic places. Remember that those girls believed in the promise of the music you could spin, in the magic of a voice and in mysteries like baseball where races are run and winners picked, every year.

PMS

Satin Worship

A notion is a "a small useful item, such as needles, buttons or thread." Thread is a notion; destiny is a thread.

Clotho spins it, Lachesis measures it, and Atropos cuts it off. They were the Fates or the *Moirai* of Greek mythology. Not only is Necessity the mother of invention, some say that Themis, Goddess of Necessity, was also the mother of the Fates. You can find depictions of Clotho ("the spinster") holding a distaff, Lachesis ("disposer of lots") with a scroll, and Atropos ("the inexorable one") with a pair of scissors. Sometimes in these depictions all three of them are hideous hags who share a single eye between them (they pass it around when they need it); in some depictions Clotho is young, Lachesis is middle-aged, and Atropos is a crone. But there are also depictions of all three as gorgeous, graceful, divine women.

That's the depiction I like best. Imbedded in it is the idea of life as raw material to be shaped into something beautiful and useful according to a woman's fancy, as well as the idea of death, not as a scary old guy with a scythe, but as a pretty goddess with a pair of very sharp scissors.

Scissors, a mundane object to which we are introduced in kindergarten (if not earlier), are a sophisticated tool requiring opposable thumbs and some dexterity. Sharp scissors are potentially a weapon; hence the instruction never to run with scissors. I imagine few homes in modern America are without at least one pair of scissors, but I also imagine that few homes are as well stocked with scissors as mine. I have kitchen scissors, several pair of paper scissors, embroidery scissors, dress-maker shears, and pinking shears.

To pink means to cut something with a decorative border; a saw-tooth zigzag edge is standard in sewing, and a way to prevent fabric from raveling. Because they have so many cutting edges, pinking shears must be kept well oiled and protected. They are also heavier than normal scissors, and not something you use everyday.

Welker

My favorite scissors are my dress-maker shears; each time I
use them, I admire not only their usefulness, but how well
made and aesthetically satisfying they are. They have a pleasing
heft, and despite that heft, the handles never pinch my thumb.
The blades open smoothly and the cuts they make are even and
crisp. The scissors are also visually appealing, made as they are
from high-quality chrome (says so right on them) and very
shiny. I keep them in a case so that the blades are protected; I
have used them for over twenty years and they have never
required sharpening—they could be a weapon easily enough.
They were a Christmas gift from my mother when I was in high
school; at the time I received them, they seemed to me an
acknowledgment that I was a pretty good seamstress, good
enough to have my own shears. I still feel a trace of pride
whenever I take them out of their case. But it occurs to me now
that my mother might also have tired of letting me borrow her
good scissors every time I wanted to cut some fabric.

Ecclesiastes 3:7 says that there is "a time to rend, and a
time to sew." I think about this every time I lay fabric on the
floor and cut out a dress. I suppose it is something of a risk—
something whole is rent—but it rarely feels like one; it feels like
a necessary step, part of a making, not an unmaking.

I love how sewing makes me feel capable and efficient.
People often ask me to mend things. "Sew this button on for
me, fix this hem, repair this ripped seam," they plead, as if
these were difficult tasks.

I would guess that needles are one of the oldest tools
humanity has invented, and there are myths to support this. In
Genesis we are told that Adam and Eve are commanded to tend
the Garden of Eden; maybe that means that they had to fashion
hoes and rakes; maybe they just used their hands. But the next
activity in which they engage is sewing aprons out of fig leaves;
that would require needles.

I've also found a book to support the antiquity of needles:
*Women's Work: the First 20,000 Years: Women, Cloth and Society in
Early Times* by Elizabeth Wayland Barber. But Barber also talks
about the antiquity of string. It had not occurred to me that
someone had to invent string, had to figure out that if you
twisted shorter, weaker filaments together, plying in new
strands as needed, you'd end up with a longer, stronger length
of cord. Seventeen-thousand-year-old string has been found
imbedded in the walls of ancient caves dwellings in southern

France. The theory is that some Paleolithic Ariadne figured out that by running a cord from cave to cave, the inhabitants could make their way through that dark labyrinth of the past.

If the Fates saw fit to cut that string, how many lives would drop away with it?

My sewing machine is a sturdy brown electric Singer, a heavy piece of cast iron. My grandmother gave it, brand new, to my mother as a high school graduation gift in 1955. I inherited it because I was the only one of my mother's four daughters with the patience to learn to read a pattern, to rip out seams when I sewed the pieces together wrong, to spend two hours pinning and hemming a dress by hand. I was the only one with fabric lust.

Calico, flannel, gaberdine, corduroy, velveteen, lace, silk, satin. I've seen a bumper sticker that reads, "Whoever dies with the most fabric, wins" and I think I'm in the running. There are two components to my fabric lust. One is pragmatic, a sense of fabric as raw material for that practical necessity, clothing. The other is admiration for something both sensual and beautiful: the smoothness of finely woven cotton or silk, the fuzzy nap of something like velvet or brushed flannel, the vividness of certain prints. I have four big bins of fabrics in various lengths, as well as a giant crate of scraps, which I sew together for quilts.

In my final year of work on a PhD in English literature, I found myself in need of both extra cash and a break from my dissertation, so I took a part-time job at a fabric store where I could get paid to fondle the fabric. The job paid barely more than minimum wage and most of the employees were part-time; hiring women who considered the job a hobby was one of the ways the company kept costs down. There were a few teachers as well as several well-to-do grandmothers, women with financial security who wanted to get out of the house for ten hours a week and be around fabric. The store was actually a fabric and craft store, but I never understood the craft aspect, why people felt compelled to buy styrofoam balls of various sizes and meld them into new objects, why someone would want to paint pre-printed designs on cheap wooden boxes, especially when there was all that fabric to be had on the other side of the store.

I liked cutting fabric for patrons well enough; it meant I could spread the fabric out, rub it between my fingers and admire the color and design, but it also meant I had to talk to the customer. Preferable was the solitary activity of putting things away. I liked stocking the notions wall. It was a truly awesome sight: a thousand square feet covered with gadgets to assist in an array of fabric-related tasks such as measuring, cutting, ironing. It was the usefulness of the notions that captivated me, and the human ingenuity that had led to their invention. Surveying that wall, it seemed to me that one could never have enough notions.

But my favorite task was reshelving the bolts of fabric after a customer had bought whatever length she needed. I would load up a shopping cart, then wander the store, looking for each bolt's place among its companion fabrics, comparing colors and wasting a moment coveting the fabrics I couldn't afford: thirty or forty or eighty dollars for a yard of full-nap 100% cotton velvet or genuine Thai silk.

The job had one primary perk: a hefty discount. More than once I spent my entire check on fabric that went straight into a storage box. I rarely had plans for the fabric I bought; it was simply beautiful, and while I did imagine that someday I would find something worthwhile to do with it, there was the more pressing imperative to *own it immediately*, five yards of that charcoal flannel, six yards of this teal and gold paisley calico.

When it came to anything but fabric I was a lousy sales person. I could help someone locate the aisle for beads or embroidery floss, but I became testy with customers who expected me to demonstrate a thorough knowledge of the details of stenciling or doll-making. I especially hated working the cash register, where I was supposed to engage in pleasant banter with people who often were buying crap that I felt shouldn't exist in the first place, and I absolutely couldn't bear that much of that crap was wrapped in excessive packaging that would end up in some landfill. The line to my register was always long, a fact the people in it always resented. "All I wanted was to buy some buttons, and I have to wait in a line like this. Can't you have a few more cashiers?" they'd ask.

"Listen, lady, I'd love it if there were a few more cashiers. But this is corporate America you're dealing with. The people in charge of decisions like that want to make money, not spend it," I'd think—sometimes I'd say it aloud. And despite the fact that I was clearly a terrible cashier, the manager seemed to think it wise to put me on cash register duty and leave me there. Once it became clear that I would be handling the cash register more than I handled fabric, I quit.

In the 1970s when I was growing up, all Mormon girls were required to study certain homemaking skills, including the fundamentals of childcare; we then had to scare up baby-sitting gigs so we could implement that knowledge. We also had to study needlework. It was part of official Church curriculum to teach 11-year-old girls to embroider and crochet; twelve-year-olds learned to knit. I never cared for embroidery; the stitches were too small and the results too purely ornamental, not at all utilitarian. I did like knitting, however. One day my grandmother saw me knitting the way I had been taught to knit at church, with a superfluous step where the yarn is wrapped by hand around the needle for the upcoming stitch, and after she recovered from her outrage, she sat me down and taught me how to do it *correctly*, by using the needles themselves to pick up a new stitch.

Knitting is a skill that has come in handy throughout my life, mostly because I am so afflicted by the Protestant work ethic that I can't bear to watch television unless I am doing something productive with my hands. I suppose in this way I am somewhat like Madame Defarge, the enigmatic matron in *A Tale of Two Cities* who sits beside the guillotine, knitting to pass the time and making a mark in her stitches for each head that is chopped off. I am a competent but not a superior knitter. My stitches, while even and smooth, are fairly tight; this makes it hard for me to do fancy stitches (not enough room to maneuver the needles inside the old stitches), but I do well with easy projects like pillows or dish towels or baby afghans. If I'm working with a simple pattern, I don't even need to look at my stitches; my hands can tell what they should be doing, and the repetitive nature of the work makes it as restful and soothing as fingering prayer beads.

Knitting is a very old activity. There was a time in European history when all peasant children learned to knit; they knit their own very scratchy underwear out of wool as well as items to sell at market. Despite its historical position as a craft of the lower classes, knitting is now rather a bourgeois activity: good yarn is anything but cheap, and the time necessary to complete something like a sweater means that you must be blessed not only with leisure, but with resolve.

I prefer to sew with cotton fabric but I would rather knit with wool; it's stretchy and forgiving. You can undo your stitches and the yarn will spring back and look smooth when you knit it again. When I bother to make something as time-intensive as a sweater, I always use wool. Cotton yarn isn't nearly so forgiving; the less expensive varieties of cotton yarn can feel like rope.

The sweaters I've made aren't impressive specimens but they've taught me a lot. If it's true that "a stitch in time saves nine," it's even truer that a stitch not in time can cost hundreds or thousands of additional stitches. One dropped stitch—a single moment's inattention—can throw an entire pattern out of whack. In a knitting class a few years ago I noticed that one of the hardest things for people to do is to take out stitches after they've made a mistake. They would rather finish a garment that has a serious flaw than go back and start over; they just keep hoping that the mistake isn't that critical, that it won't show. They can't bear to have their time rendered a waste by dint of a mistake and would rather commit to continuing flawed article than to just starting over. And so they waste more time and more yarn and end up with something they can't even use.

I make a lot of baby quilts, partly because I know a lot of people who have babies, and partly because a baby quilt is a gratifyingly manageable project. You can design the pattern and sew together all the blocks for the top in a weekend. Furthermore, the sandwich of fabric backing, batting and patchworked-quilt-top with which you work is small enough that you can easily hold it on your lap and keep it taut with a quilting hoop rather than having to stretch it out on a frame that could fill an entire room.

Quilting refers to stitching all the layers together; things can be hand- or machine-quilted, stitched with elaborate patterns or simple lines. I consider quilting one of the most artistic things I do. I'm not much good at drawing but I have a decent eye for color and shape; I always design my own quilts, and I can tell when a pattern needs a dark block here, a light one there. Someone once asked me to show her all the quilts I've made. "I gave them away," I said, surprised. "I made them as gifts."

"Didn't you take pictures of them first?" she asked. But I didn't, any more than I took pictures of dresses I made before I wore them.

Spinning a yarn is a metaphor for *telling a story,* and stories can be *embroidered.* But quilting doesn't seem to be of much use as a way to talk about narrative. Stitching contrasting pieces of fabric into a pattern, stitching that to another piece of fabric with some stuffing in the middle so that heat-trapping pockets of air are formed—that's too elaborate for the way our culture likes to talk about writing. In fact, it's rather an insult to call a story a *patchwork,* but high praise to call it *seamless.*

I was commanded to learn a lot of home-making skills; I acquired the skills but not the home, not in the way I was supposed to, anyway. My skills are not put to use in service of a husband and children of my own. In fact I am what you might call a *spinster aunt.* My four siblings have provided me with over a dozen nieces and nephews. The term spinster originally meant *one who spins,* though it has come to mean an *old maid,* someone who has womanly attributes but whose womanhood is not fully realized.

I've seen spinning wheels, in museums and in photos, but I've never handled one, and I want to. I want to learn to spin fibers into thread. If nothing else, I think it would help me understand what's going on the next time I encounter a fairy tale where a maiden is required to spin or caught at her spinning or killed because she pricks her finger on a spindle. I've seen a drawing of the Venus de Milo with arms—and they're in the right position for spinning. I'm intrigued by the way *spinning* has equaled *women* throughout history, and by the vestiges of that notion in our culture. For instance, while the patrilineal side of a family is known as the "spear side," the matrilineal side is called the "distaff side," a distaff being a wooden board, sometimes plain but often intricately carved, to which the raw material to be spun (flax, wool, cotton) is tied, and from which the spinner draws as she winds the thread or yarn onto a spindle or wheel.

For many, many centuries, the average person would have been familiar with the complex processes by which fiber becomes clothing, having either observed or engaged in the processes herself: first the fiber is carded and spun. It can be dyed before or after it is woven. It can be cut and sewn together in shapes resembling the body, and it can then be embroidered, beaded, pleated, smocked, quilted, painted, sequined, bejeweled.

Fabric stimulates several of our senses. It can be any color, shiny or matte, patterned or plain; its texture can be soft or silky or fuzzy or nubby or fluffy. Fabric can even appeal to the ear: there is the crinkle of a stiff fabric like taffeta or the rough sound of corduroy rubbing against itself. Textiles can be utilitarian, sensual, expressive, beautiful and extravagant all at once.

For millennia, textiles have served as a metaphor for both an entire gender and an individual life. Even when the myth that spinning women controlled the fates of humanity was abandoned, the idea that *spinning = women* hung on. Spinning is now a task done by machines, not real women, and so spinning is now associated with a form of counterfeit womanhood. Well, I'm not afraid of working with my hands or of old maidenhood. I'm trying to spin and weave the fibers of my life into a tapestry both beautiful and useful, and of my own design.

HERE IN IRAQ

In setting out to write about being a female in the military, I find it quite difficult to differentiate between my thoughts and feelings and those of my male counterparts. I am a female. I am a part of the United States Army. I am serving my country as a soldier in Baghdad. I am just one of thousands. Life here is difficult for all people.

Having been here for eight months and counting, I have seen and experienced more things than most 22-year-old college students ever will. I have developed and matured as a student, soldier, a daughter, and a Christian. For all of these things, I am grateful.

As a student of history, I have always read about war, oppression, dictatorships, and nation-building. My, what a history class this has been. I will never be the same after this. I will be better. My heart, mind, and spirit have all been opened.

Despite the destruction, poverty, and death all around, I find happiness here. I see smiling children waving as we pass. I see mothers proudly carrying their newborns. I see wedding parties with decorated cars, music, and laughter. I see vivid murals being painted on bridges and buildings. I see progress being made.

Being a female soldier working in a male-dominated country has been quite an interesting experience. Female soldiers here get attention. The Iraqis literally stop what they are doing to watch us. The men, women, and children all stare. It would probably be the same response as if a nudist were walking nonchalantly through the streets back in Alabama. Something quite out of the ordinary.

Many simply just do not understand why there are female soldiers doing the same jobs as males. To see a woman uncovered, in pants, with a weapon, or driving, is quite uncommon. And all of these things at once—wow. Imagine the reactions. Nonetheless, despite the many glances and extra attention received, most Iraqis have been respectful, especially the children. The children are even more intrigued by us than the

81

adults. They are wonderful, happy, and sincere, just like children everywhere.

Here in Iraq, I introduce myself as Miriam, which is a common name here. It is a beautiful name and I've grown quite fond of it. All the children call me "Mrs. Miriam," which always brings a smile to my face.

During the first six months of our deployment our company worked at three police stations in the southern districts of Baghdad. Being summer, when school was out, there were always children gathered around the stations. Some lived next door, some worked with their parents nearby, and a few even took a cab over just to be around the Americans. They would sell us soft drinks, ice cream (pronounced "icy cream"), ice, and "finger chips," which is what they call French fries. When it was 130 degrees, ice and cold drinks were hard to come by and always a welcomed treat. The children would come up with their beverages saying, "Six for one dollar!" which sounded more like "sex for one dollar," and always brought a chuckle from us.

Many of the younger children know bits of English which they were always eager to use. With the influx of satellite television in Iraq now, which was banned under Saddam's regime, the children are exposed to more English. They of course pick up words and phrases from the American soldiers as well. They know the most important words: humvee, hot, water, food, Pepsi, M16, helicopter, gum, and give-me. It's amazing how far those few words can go in conversation. They also knew the most important Americans: George Bush, Britney Spears, and Michael Jackson.

The older children, who had been educated, usually knew English from school. It was so interesting talking to them.

Journal entry from August 20, 2003:
"I haven't seen any children in over a week. I miss them. I miss the sounds of their voices, their laughter, the spark in the eyes, their innocence. No longer do I see the world as a happy place where all is beautiful. I have lost that childish innocence. When I showed Mustafa and Ahmed a picture of Santa Claus last week, they said, "Santa Claus dead, Saddam killed him." All those years when we were told that Santa visits all the children in the world and brings happiness everywhere, and it was all a lie.

Sometimes I feel the same way now in looking at this desperate place that I felt when I learned Santa Claus wasn't real. Maybe it would be better never even to believe in a Santa Claus, or a peaceful world. The children here don't. But then again, that's what made childhood so wonderful, believing in good things and the fairy tales. I wonder what the children here believe in. What do they dream about?"

Most of the women we see are fully clothed in loosely fitting black garments with their heads covered. Usually their entire face is showing, but sometimes just their eyes. Generally, the women we see are carrying food to their homes, going to the market, or out working in the fields. They appear very stern, tough, and hard-working. They all seem to age quickly.

I remember the first time I saw women in prison here.

Journal entry from September 14, 2003:
"The IP's (Iraqi police) had just brought in three prisoners who had been arrested for car-jacking and murder. They had car-jacked a male and beat him so severely that he had died of his injuries in the hospital. The IP's had caught them in the act and shot one of the suspects. They arrested the other two men and the female, who they had just brought in. They put the female in a cell, then proceeded to beat the males.

The IP's said that the men would be executed for murder but the woman would not. She was placed in a cell with another female and would be released upon a payment. The other female was in jail for prostitution. Strange. I had never even fathomed that that would be a problem in this society, but evidently that has been a worldwide problem throughout history.

The prostitute looked like a typical Iraqi woman, covered with her black burka, accompanied in the cell by her nursing baby. She would be held for two days then released. However, she is married. After her family and husband were informed of what she had done, they said that if she came back home, she would be killed. The interpreter said there are many females arrested for murder, prostitution, and thieving. Who would have thought? I wondered what would happen to her, and what would happen to her baby."

At our old compound, where we lived up until just a month ago, we saw it improve tremendously. When we arrived in

Baghdad on June 28, 2003, after spending a month in tents in the Kuwaiti desert, Camp Graceland, as we came to call it, seemed like a dump.

It was an abandoned, looted, industrial warehouse. There were no windows, doors, ceiling tiles, or fixtures. There was no water or power. More importantly there was no air conditioning (we wouldn't get any until mid-August). There was trash everywhere, broken glass, concrete, and layers of oil and grime. What a feeling to stand there, not knowing where to start cleaning, and having reality set in that this is to be home for the next few months. (or so we naively thought) Had we known at that point that we would be here for 365 days, I'm not sure we would have handled it as well.

Nonetheless, with plenty of patience, time, and hajji workers, Camp Graceland became a decent home. The females, 16 of us, were given one room and each of us had our nice 7-foot by 4-foot area to ourselves. I'm not sure if I cried the first night there, but if not, I should have. Looking back on it now though, I'm able to smile. People moving in now have no idea what it used to be like; words simply cannot do it justice.

I digress on the topic of hajji workers. Now I'm not sure who exactly began calling Iraqis "hajjis," but that has simply become a standard part of the military jargon here in Iraq. The word Hajj refers to the holy pilgrimage to Mecca made by the Muslims who are able to go. From this word Hajj derives the term hajji which refers to one who has made the aforesaid trip. However, among U.S. soldiers, it is used to describe most Iraqi workers and merchants as well as an adjective to describe merchandise bought from such merchants and shops. Example: Most military compounds now have at least one hajji shop with hajji sandwiches and hajji DVD's. Many also have hajji internet, an internet café run by hajji workers.

Now I have heard that this is a derogatory, politically incorrect term, a sort of racial slang. But I have asked many Iraqis if they were offended by this, to which they replied, "No." So I continue to use this term with a clear conscience.

So, the military hires hajjis to do all sorts of work around our compounds. They build, clean, sew, launder, cook, and bring us all sorts of items to spend our money on. We need work done and they need jobs, so it works out well for all involved.

I often wonder what they think of working for Americans. What do they think of us?

Journal entry from September 7, 2003:
"I stopped by the softball game for a few minutes. Since the
weather has been a bit cooler, some of the guys have been playing pick up games with other companies. At the start of the
game, many of the hajji workers were waiting on their rides, so
they were all standing around waiting. They were all intently
watching the game and all of us. I wonder what they were
thinking. I bet for them, stepping into this compound is a bit
like stepping into the USA. Though in Iraq, we have
'Americanized' everything as best we could. They see all of our
pictures of families, homes pets, friends, cars, boats, schools,
and everything else we put on our walls.

They see all the food we have here, all the walkmans, CD's,
cameras, DVD players, DVD's, books, and games. To them, this
place is probably luxurious.

The hajjis watched them play ball almost as if they were
amazed to see us enjoying ourselves. They see us on the roads
in full battle rattle, war faces on, loaded weapons. Then they
come here and see us playing games, sleeping, eating, watching
movies and trying to have some fun. They are the few Iraqis
who see this side of us. They see that we aren't all the big bad
Americans we try to act like-we're just people, just like them.

As much as I observe and make notes of being here in their
world, when they come here, they probably have even more
culture shock. I wonder what they go home and tell their families about us."

Journal entry from September 8, 2003:
"When are we going home? The question we've all been asking
since we stepped foot in the Middle East, was finally answered
today. There was a general from the National Guard Bureau
that came and had a meeting with all Guard commanders. He
said that we would be here for 365 days in theatre, meaning
that none of our time at Fort Benning counted. We will be on
active duty for 15 months total. Not good news. Everyone is
frustrated. That seems like an eternity. How will the situation
here be then? Better? Worse? Who knows?

But whatever the date, I'll still make it home and try and
pick up where I left off. Though of course my life will never be
the same and I won't be picking up exactly everything. I'm sure
I won't be hanging out with all the same people nor doing all
the same things. I will have to re-evaluate who I consider my

true friends. I will look at people differently, be a little more appreciative, spend more time with family, and spend more time relaxing. I will think a bit differently about America, foreign policy, the United Nations, the military, Islam, terrorism, and Iraq. I'm sure that I will think about Iraq at least once every day for the rest of my life. I'm sure it will be a main topic of conversation months after I am home.

I know people will look at me and wonder what it was like; the same way I look at veterans with a sense of wonder and amazement of the things they've done and seen. I look at them differently than all other people, with a deepest respect, because I know they have experienced things that no one will ever understand. They have thought, analyzed, and reflected upon things that most people never will. They know more about themselves, the world, and America, than most Americans do. They deserve all the respect given them. I hope I too will be given that respect and that I will make people wonder what I've experienced. I want people to look at me differently because I am different. And no one but those like us will ever understand why we are different."

poemmemoir**story**

CLAIRVOYANT

My name is Clarence Day, and my parents were normal. That's what it says on my traveling van right after it says, in perfect red letters, that I'm 20" high and weigh 39 lbs., THE WORLD'S SMALLEST MAN. It also says I have a high school education. When that got added to the sign, my income went up 17%. My wife did that calculation, she keeps the books. It doesn't say so on the sign, but she's normal too. The loudspeaker tells about her once we've settled in at the fairgrounds and opened up for business. I hear over and over again, maybe eighty times a day, that I have a normal wife and two perfectly normal children. One of them collects the money while the other one hangs around a lot and calls me Dad. We all work together, and we eat well.

You're probably wondering if those two boys are really my children. People want to know that but they never ask. I guess there's just no way to ask that question and feel good about yourself. If someone could figure a nice way to ask, I'd tell the truth. I'm pretty sure they're mine—as sure as any man is. I don't think about it much.

I'm good at my job. The sign says I'm small, and I am. I don't cheat people, even though they think I do. When they see me, I can tell they expected more for their 50 cents. I guess they expect a perfect little man, a tiny mirror of themselves, a little doll. They don't expect the head and trunk of a midget (even though they have to admit I'm a very small midget) with vestigial legs. But that's what they get. I'm not a doll. And nothing is perfect, not even freaks.

To be honest, I don't enjoy my work like I used to. Used to be that I'd hear footsteps on the wooden platform outside my trailer and my stomach would tighten as I waited for the faces to appear at the door—confident, happy faces on their day off, all lit up with the expectation of seeing something they could talk about back home on the front porch with a cool pitcher of lemonade sitting by. That wasn't the part I enjoyed, not that I begrudged it or anything. I liked the next part, the sudden bewilderment when those faces took account that it wasn't just them seeing me but I was seeing them right back again. They hadn't reckoned on that when they paid their 50 cents, and I could see the sweat come up, see the eyes check for escape routes. I had them then—the world belonged to me in those moments they were recalculating, and I could have sent it spinning out of control. They were mine, and for a split second they almost were me, I was that real to them. But I did nothing, of course. I just watched and enjoyed those moments until they got control of themselves again and said hello, clearing their throats of the fear that had got lodged there. We could chat then, with the touching formality of strangers who have survived a crisis together.

The chat hasn't changed. How do? Think there might be rain coming on? Hope not. Left the windows open back t'home. Ain't rained all month—be just my luck to have it coming in the windows the one day me and the family step out some. Ain't that always the way. Same conversations I've been having all my life, in uncertain weather. Rain and sun mean minor adjustments. Some folks don't put high value on that kind of chat, think nothing's getting said. But from where I sit, it seems like more's being said than any creature can take stock of. People come in there to see me and, no matter how disappointed they are, I expect they remember me a good long while. I expect what they remember, what pulls their coats every now and again, is the questions they didn't ask, that I didn't answer. Same thing I remember about them, all of them, and it's a lot to remember from so much chat, so many unanswered questions.

Could be I'm getting weary from so much remembering. Maybe that's where the salt's gone. Could be time for me to move on, do some other work. It's not always that I've worked the fairgrounds here in upstate Alabama, not by a long shot. It was some thirty years ago that we first settled on the outskirts of Gadsden. Had us an old farmhouse in those days, and a yellow Packard, a clear and shiny yellow that nature never thought of, unless you think people are natural. Every time I looked at that Packard I got hungry for sweets. Gained four pounds the year we got it, four delicious pounds that made me sick and happy. In those days we had a makeshift wagon, a box on wheels is what it was, that we'd hook up to the Packard on work days. Thinking back on it, I guess that box was real paltry. We painted it with at least twenty different shades of yellow, but next to the Packard it was nothing but dull and puny. No light inside except what came through the door and the chinks in the wood. When folks came in to see me, they were really thrown off balance. Face to face with a freak in a dark box, nothing else to look at and no place to run. Pretty near all the men and women who walked through that door wished they hadn't, wished they could vanish back out into the sunlight in the blink of an eye. But every single one of them stayed for at least a minute or two. It wasn't the money they'd paid that made them do it, it was their pride. It's human pride that's kept me in business all these years, and I'm mighty thankful for it.

Things are different now. You step in the door it's almost like stepping into somebody's living room. There's carpeting, electric lights, a kitchenette. Even upholstered chairs if people want to sit down. Most prefer standing. Still, that old box on wheels had some magic in it. Maybe magic is the price you pay for comfort.

We gave up the farmhouse, too, for a split-level ranch-style, indoor-outdoor carpet, 29" color tv, furniture from Ethan Allen. It's more than comfortable. Funny how most folks just assume we live right here in the trailer, all four of us and not a bed in sight. Nice place you got here, they say, meaning nice home. But usually they ask if I come from around these parts—my accent isn't quite right, although I try—and I say, sure do, have a split-level just southeast of Gadsden. That's all they need to hear.

They also like to ask how long I've been married. I say forever, and they laugh. So I laugh too. But I don't let it stop there like I do with the weather. I go on and tell them that she's the finest woman on the face of the earth, and that's a fact. They look over at her—she's always right there—and I can see her in their eyes, see a normal woman flash up on their eyeballs. Then comes the squint, barely perceptible, while they wonder—wonder what it's like between me and her. Behind those eyes there's a quick parade of snapshots—her and me at the dinner table, in the living room, in the bed. Finest woman on earth, I repeat, and the eyes come back to me. That's when I stop. I don't say that when we lie down together I'm tall.

Being the world's smallest man is my job. It's my work, and we all have to work one way or another. I do my job well, but doing it poorly would be just as much work, probably more.

There were some folks walked through my door just last week, young folks just starting to get the feel of being on their own. You have to admire the courage it takes to get the feel of that. Whatever else the young ones do or don't have, they've got courage. It's as common as the sparrow, and no less precious. Well, these kids are larking, and they come busting in the door full of fresh air and junk food and high spirit, till the hush settles on them. Four of them there are, and who's going to speak up first? You know they can't take too much of the hush. The guy that's first through the door stops short two steps in, causing a jam-up at his rear, so they're all stuck there together, a single lump of young humanity with eight big eyes. I never speak first.

Hi.

The sweetest sound you can imagine, and we're all grateful. Hi back to you, I say, with the emphasis on *to*. Come on in if you'd like. They separate out into two girls and two boys. The girl that said hi walks right up to me, Young Mr. First doesn't budge, and the other two shuffle in line between them. Where you folks from? I'm from Birmingham, says Hi, and I see myself in her eyes big as life. Bigger. I look down the line, getting smaller and smaller, and I say you sure did pick a nice day to come to the fair. Mr. First has his eyes on my wife already, wondering, and Hi says yeah, it's real nice out there. She's worried now, doesn't want me to think she meant it isn't nice in here, so she asks if I come from around here. You know what I say, about the split-level outside Gadsden. Oh, she says, you don't sound like you're from Alabama. I say, you wouldn't believe all the places I've been in my life, telling her the truth. How'd you end up here? she asks. (My wife speaks up, says the kids are going out for hamburgers. Do I want one? No, I'm not hungry just yet, thank you.) I don't have to answer the question now, but I do. I say it's a good place to work. She wants to know why but doesn't ask, trying to figure it out for herself. Mr. First down there is thinking, what does this dwarf know about work, sitting around on his tiny can all day, talking shit and collecting money? He's thinking about how hard he works, stashing all the goddamn pork loins and margarine and kotex into the goddamn bags for a bunch of old hags who don't even give him a goddamn tip. And here he is spending 50 cents to see a dwarf sit on his can.

He's right, of course. He works hard, too hard. It's a crying shame anyone's got to work as hard as he does, and it's a job to figure what makes them do it. It's not the money like he thinks it is. Twenty years from now he'll be rolling in money, eating tenderloin and lying down each night with a woman who does-n't tip the grocery sackers. And he'll still be working too hard. I won't be here then, but when he drives past the fairgrounds I'll be bile in his belly. His eyes will narrow in remembrance of the little fucker who sat on his can for a living.

On down the row, the skinny fellow with curly hair—it's brown in here but outside I know it's been golden—is looking at me in the past tense. I'm a story he's telling one Thursday night at Dugan's, story about a city boy venturing up a forlorn stretch of 1-59 to experience the carnival of life among yester-day's people. His friends are enjoying the story, and so am I. He sets it up real good: the sunlight glinting off his Honda Civic in a field of unwashed pick-ups, the arduous journey from the parking lot through rows of pit-bulls and coon hounds that are bought and sold by dangerous characters (he describes them—big bellies, no teeth, huge biceps; oddly cordial, even gracious, but scary as shit, like dams that could burst any minute and ravage everything in their path), the tables piled high with stolen hubcaps and ghetto blasters next to a table with nothing to sell but two rusted kettles and a broken toaster (Westinghouse, 1961). In the midst of it all a preacher, a kid in a J.C. Penney double-knit suit stained with his sweat, yelling about Gawd and Cheesus. Gathered around him are eight slack-jawed farmers in overalls but no shirts, all twice the age of the preacher but awed, respectful, nodding as he tells them—begs them—to bring prayer into their lives and prepare for the com-ing of the Lorrrr-d—"For I say unto you, my brothers (hunh), that just as you put on your socks in the morning (hunh) before you go to put on your shoes (hunh), you must put on the Lorrrr-d, my brothers (hunh), before you can enter His Kingdom (hunh). The Kingdom awaits you, my brothers (hunh), but you have to dress rightly (hunh). Put on Cheesus every morning, brothers (hunh), and you'll march to Jerusalem (hunh) in Gawd's very own shoes…" (A dramatic pause from our young storyteller here, and a giggle.) Suddenly a small pro-jectile rebounds off the sweaty sleeve of the double-knit suit. In the booth next door a man is throwing chocolate ex-lax into the passing crowd—chocolate ex-lax, for chrissake—and people are down on their knees scooping the stuff up. You can tell the old farmers are tempted but don't want to be rude to the preacher, who's ignoring the ex-lax as best he can. (The crowd at Dugan's is laughing, but the story could be better, still needs work.) Finally, at the edge of the fairgrounds is this big yellow trailer with a banner on the side that says THE WORLD'S SMALLEST MAN / CLARENCE DAY / 20" HIGH / 39 LBS / NORMAL PARENTS / HIGH SCHOOL DIPLOMA / ADMISSION 50 CENTS. This voice is squawking on a loudspeaker about this guy's got a normal wife and two perfectly normal kids. I see a blond-headed kid, looks just like my little brother, hanging off the door, asking his dad for lunch money. Vick didn't want to go in, said it was all bullshit hype, but Nancy and I paid our 50 cents and you know Vick, wouldn't be caught missing anything and starts acting like it was his idea in the first place. Pays for both him and Rose and we all go in. (Pause) I don't know what I was expecting, but, man, it was *weird*. (How was it weird?— this story's losing momentum, it isn't going anywhere.) I mean, it's like a normal room in there, little lamps and chairs, curtains on the window. There's a woman standing by the refrigerator, a plain woman, not bad looking, about my height. But right in the middle there's this box-like thing, like a little stage sort of but more like a little barn with one wall missing, and that's where the world's smallest man is, looking right at us, very casual as if…as if this was just an ordinary thing. It's kind of hard to describe but, I mean we were supposed to be looking at him but he was looking at us and just kind of like, well, *waiting*. I mean he was a real disappointment in a way. Vick was right, I guess—he was just a regular midget with no legs. With legs he'd have been normal height, for a midget, so it was like cheating. But it was weird. (*How?*) I mean, we had this perfectly normal conversation, very boring really, but it was a strange experience. I can't describe it.

And finally he stops trying. There's something good here, he thinks, something about the South, about human nature and values, something that will make people laugh in just the right way. But he can't quite get it. It needs more work. He orders a rum and coke, feeling distracted and uneasy, but nobody seems to notice.

I like the storyteller. Next time he'll edit me out and be a big success, but he'll keep knowing I'm there, wondering how to tell it right. Right now, looking down at me in the trailer, he's pleased with his story and the day's outing.

The other girl…well, she's having a hard time dealing with this and would rather not. It's gotten real hot in here all of a sudden, and there's a musty smell—not a particularly bad smell, but she feels herself breathing it in and doesn't want it inside of her. If she'd known what it was like, she'd have stayed outside. Can't imagine why anyone pays money to be uncomfortable like this. The only right thing to do in here is stare at this poor little man, but out on the street it would be the wrong thing to do. It's impolite to stare at the handicapped, not very pleasant either. She remembers going with her mother to the dimestore when she was a kid. A lady was there at the lunch counter eating a hamburger and she had this huge lump on her neck, like a balloon that got stuck to her face from the cheekbone down to the collar bone and the skin had just grown right over it. Her mom was busy fingering through the cosmetics display, and Rose just stared at that lump, hands clenched at her sides, afraid to feel her own face. As the lady chewed her hamburger, the lump didn't move at all—it was solid and still. The whole world narrowed in on that lump and that hamburger. The smell of the hamburger. Rose threw up all over the floor of the dimestore and didn't feel right again for days. God must have a reason for doing this to people, maybe so the rest of us could count our blessings that He could have done it to us but didn't. Well, she sure does feel blessed, but it's not right to stare at people who aren't.

My wife is checking Rose out pretty close. Every once in a while we have folks getting sick in here—we've even had a few faint on us—and, believe me, it ruins our day as well as theirs. I'm hoping these kids are out of here before Todd gets back with the burgers, when suddenly Nancy asks, what's it like?

You can tell she's surprised she asked it and spooked now that it's out. She glances at Vick and Rose, who are wishing they didn't know her. Daniel lost the drift somewhere and doesn't know what she's asking. Fact is, she isn't sure either. Well, I'm on the spot now. I could say pretty near anything and it would be true, but what's the best truth for her and me right now? Nothing rises up to say itself like her question did. I have to choose an answer, and I want to do a good job. That's it, of course, so I tell her that it's a job. It's what I do, and I try to do it well. Right away I recognize that I haven't gotten through to her, I've just gotten us both off the spot. The weariness comes on me, and I wish it didn't have to be like this. I wish I could open up her head and put the answer inside, put myself inside, and sleep. And sleep. I think I know what it's like to sleep, but I

can't say I remember doing it myself. I close my eyes sometimes, but I don't see less clearly. Fact is I see more clearly, not
just the upholstered chairs and lamps, the wife and kids, but
lawns and battlefields, rug salesmen, princesses, outhouses,
astrolabes, Walter the Penniless, Jane Fonda, broken scissors
and Faberge' eggs. Some folks say they have trouble remembering things, but the real trouble is forgetting. When those four
kids said their good-byes last week and filed on out of the trailer, they marched right into the thick of my memories, and
they'll stay there forever, rubbing elbows with people they
don't even know about. At least not yet. They're still young
now, and they think their lives are their own, but they're wrong
about that. They're mine, too, and—like it or not—I'm theirs.
That's what they got for their 50 cents. What I got was four
new voices.

RESERVOIR

It's the summer before I start college and I walk miles every day. "Where do you go, Lynn?" my mother asks. Nowhere, everywhere. I just keep walking. Sometimes I walk the perimeter of town and sometimes I walk up and down the streets. I might start with a north-south pattern and after a few hours switch to east-west. I know every house in Banfield, the cars in the driveways, the mailboxes, the dogs. I look at everything but I never slow down. One foot in front of the other, on and on until it's time to go home for dinner. After eating, I sit on the couch and watch television until I know I can fall asleep.

I wear black leather boots that reach mid-calf under my jeans. The summer heat is miserable, my feet roast, but I wear these boots every day. I take them off just before I go to bed at night and stand them where I can reach them immediately when I wake. My mother complains that they smell, asks me how I can stand such nasty foot odor, but I just shrug. The soles have a lot of wear left and that's all that matters.

My best friend, Carolanne, doesn't know what to make of me. We've spent every previous summer swimming at the reservoir and playing tennis. For high school graduation, she got her father's old Mustang convertible. We should be cruising Main Street, wearing shades and pretending to be small town celebrities. But all I want to do is walk.

The reservoir has an airy green smell. It's the green scent of summer, of chlorophyll, of rampant photosynthesis. The sun loses its way trying to penetrate the dense leaves of the trees that ring the water. And the water itself is dark and thick and green, absorbing the sweat and energy of the swimmers.

Last summer, Carolanne and I headed for the reservoir every day after lunch. The water was warm but still felt fresh. We started by swimming laps but eventually just floated on our backs or treaded water. Our friends from high school were there and we talked in the water just like we talked around the lunch table in the cafeteria. The guys were always trying to outdo each others' dives, to see who could make the biggest splash. Hank Attelby's chest and face were always tinged red from his colossal belly flops. When he landed near us, spraying our faces, I called out, "Give it a rest!"

Hank's cousin, Billy Lockwood, was visiting from Tulsa. There were rumors that his father had died in a freak accident at an oil refinery and that Billy was more than his mother could handle. Grief-stricken, she sent her son to live with her sister's family while she raised Billy's two younger sisters. Hank bragged that his cousin had spent a night in jail when he was only fourteen for hot-wiring a car and joy-riding all over Tulsa. He'd been suspended from school three times before his mother threw up her hands and packed his bags. But Hank exaggerated; I didn't know what to believe.

Billy dated someone new every week. It caused a lot of quarrels among the girls. Friends fought over him and got in a snit whenever he showed up at the reservoir with a different girl, sometimes one who was younger than us and hardly deserving. As we treaded water, we gossiped about how insipid the girl was, what questionable taste Billy had. Mary Ellen Beamen said she'd heard that he only wanted one thing, and that when he didn't get it, he moved on and tried his luck with someone else. My friends judged him harshly, but I never bad-mouthed him. I was a virgin, but I thought I understood Billy because of my secret.

My secret. Something I'd never reveal to anyone. While in the reservoir, with my arms stretched on either side of me, I pedaled in the water as if riding a bike. The movement caused a yearning between my legs that I learned to answer. The expression on my face didn't give me away. I kept up the conversation with Carolanne and our friends, no one privy to the excitement occurring beneath the opaque water. Over and over I pedaled, my wet thighs rubbing together until I was throbbing with joy. If that's how Billy felt, if his body asked a question that had to be answered, I understood.

Throughout high school, my dark blonde hair hung in heavy waves to my shoulders. Usually I tied it back in a ponytail. But today, while out on one of my endless walks, I stop at the barber shop and ask him to cut it off.

"How much, sweetheart?" he asks.

"All of it."

I see his reflection in the mirror, the way he spikes his eye-brows and creases his lips. "You want me to take it *all* off?"

"Yes. Cut it all off. I want it as short as yours."

For a half hour I sit perfectly still as the barber snips locks of hair that fall silently to the floor, a soundless heap of dead protein. When he starts to remove the smock, I say, "NO!" my voice so forceful he cups his ears. "Take it *all* off. I want it this long," I say, indicating about a half-inch between my thumb and forefinger. When the barber finally finishes, I can't believe how ugly I look, how misshapen my head seems, how large and protruding my ears are. "Thank you," I say simply as I step down from the chair, "I'll be back for a trim in a couple weeks."

I've known Hank Attelby since the third grade when he trans-ferred from public school to St. John the Baptist Elementary. He's been our paper boy since junior high. I always suspected he had a crush on me by the way he blushed whenever we spoke. He was in the middle crowd, not popular but not an out-cast. There just wasn't anything special about him. Until his cousin arrived.

Every girl had her eye on Billy. Yes, he was new and that made him special, but he also had black hair and wild blue eyes and an easy, offhand manner. His popularity with the girls earned him grudging respect among the guys. Hank rode Billy's coattails and was suddenly one of us. Unless you live in a small town, you just can't understand how rare it is that someone, anyone, gets a shot at being something different than he's been all along. The transition was too fast; we expect-ed Hank to be more humble about his rise in status, but he acted like he'd been one of us all along. He dated Billy's cast-offs and started going steady with Susie Maxwell, a majorette in the marching band. When he saw me at the reservoir, he hollered out my last name, *"Dundee!"* like we were on equal footing. But he was the same old Hank as far as I was concerned.

I was in my backyard stretched out on a lawn chair reading a book one afternoon when he snuck up behind me and untied the back of my bikini top. As I jerked my head around, I saw the self-satisfied smirk on his face. He had rolled up our news-paper into a cylinder, and then he smacked my behind with it, not hard, but I was indignant.

"Catching some rays, Lynn?"

Laying on my stomach, I was having a hard time re-tying the back of my suit. I couldn't get up for fear he'd glimpse my breasts. My clumsy position frustrated me. "Get lost," I said, pretending to go back to my reading.

I must have stunned him because he paused before saying, "What's with you? Can't take a little joke?"

"Ha, ha," I said dryly. "You can leave now, paper boy."

I heard him sigh and start to leave. He turned back, though, and said, "You're not as cool as you think."

Slowly, I turned my head to look at him. I let my eyes run down and up his body, a cool appraisal, and said, "Yeah? And where would you be without Billy?"

He did leave then. I heard the large wheels of his heavy newspaper wagon grinding with frustration down our gravel driveway.

After I got my hair cut short, I began to eat. At first I would take a break while walking and stop for a milkshake, but now I'm carrying a backpack filled with candy bars and Oreos. While eating dinner with my family, I eat slowly, filling up my plate again and again. I'm always the last to leave the table. My little brother protests it's so I won't have to do the dishes and he will. At first my mother is flattered; I have never praised her cooking before, and she wanted me to put some weight on. But now the pounds are adding up, and she's making comments like, "College fellas don't like a girl who's on the chunky side," and, as I gain even more weight, "Lynn, if you don't stop eating like this, you're going to look like the side of a barn!"

"Leave her be," my father interrupts. He says so little, this surprised us all, and even I have to stop chewing for a moment to glance at him. He's dipping his bread in gravy, his face turned downward. Her lips tight, my mother takes her dish to the sink and drops it. The ringing sound of the stoneware plate against the porcelain sink vibrates for several moments. She opens the kitchen door and sits on the stoop, the smell of resentful cigarette smoke reaching us within moments.

Later that night, my mother walks in my room and shuts the door. Leaning against it, she pulls her lips into her mouth. I'm sitting on the bed about to pull my boots off. When she doesn't say anything, I look at her and say, "What?"

She rolls her head against the door and looks at the ceiling.

"Tell me," she whispers, "just tell me. Are you one of those...
lesbians?"

I didn't think my mother even knew the word, and I burst
out laughing. Immediately relieved, she laughs too, glad to
think that I find her question absurd. I don't know when it happens, but I realize I'm not laughing any more. I'm crying,
mountainous sobs trapped in my throat.

"What is it Lynn, what is it?" she asks, frightened. She walks
towards me and sits next to me on the bed. "What is going on
with you? Your hair and all this eating? Walking all over town
like some kind of gypsy? Just what's going on?"

The skin on my face is slick with moisture. I run my fingers
over my cheeks and slip them in my mouth, the taste of the salt
biting my tongue. I wish I could eat my sobs.

"Is there something you're not telling me? What's *wrong*
with you?"

Her last question slays me and my cries become silent, air
rushing from me in heaving breaths.

Mother persists: "Lynn! People are talking!" She pulls
my fingers from my mouth and examines them with puzzled
disgust.

I lay down on my bed, turning on my side so I don't have
to look at her. Finally I manage to say, "I'm tired. I want to go
to sleep."

Billy Lockwood had beautiful form. His running dives into the
reservoir were fast and graceful. There was a moment when he
flew above the water, his arms fanned like the wings of a con-
dor, before he tilted forward and brought his hands over his
head. Whenever he dived, the whole reservoir became quiet.
After he splashed beneath the surface, we went back to treading
water and talking. And I moved my thighs together again, the
water slipping like silk against my skin.

When Billy grabbed my foot under the water one day, I panicked. I wondered if he had discovered my secret, if he was
going to tell everyone. But then he bobbed up and said, "Race
you across. Last one there's a rotten egg!"

It was the most attention he'd paid to me and I took off
swimming after him. He got to the other side way before me
but he stood on the bank and offered me his hand. "You're cute
for a rotten egg," he said. We sat on the bank the rest of the
afternoon and talked. Carolanne kept shooting me glances that I

101

ignored. You could hear a buzzing of voices as everyone at the reservoir sized up me and Billy, wondering what to make of us.

It was flattering having his total attention. His buddies kept trying to interrupt our conversation, but he'd just nod at them and say, "Later." When he asked me to go to the drive-in movie with him that night, I told him he could pick me up at seven.

He was driving Hank's father's old car, a rusted Chevy station wagon that had one of the back doors tied shut. But the front seat was roomy and at the drive-in he slid over next to me and slipped his arm around my shoulders.

"You're the prettiest girl in Banfield," he whispered.

I rolled my eyes. "You'll have to do better than that."

He blinked slowly, popping his eyes comically, and I guessed that most girls just ate up everything he said. "Okay, how's this? The only reason I didn't ask you out when I first hit town was Hank told me he had his eye on you."

"That's better." I pressed my shoulders into the upholstery. "But he and Susie seem pretty cozy these days."

"Yeah, he and Susie-Q are quite the couple." He reached around into the back seat and set a six-pack of Rolling Rock onto the seat beside him. The previews started to come on the drive-in screen and noise blared in the speaker we had positioned in the window. I turned the volume down until almost all the static was gone.

"You've got quite a reputation," I said.

"Who, me?"

I gave him a smart-aleck look and he chuckled. "Yeah? What're they saying?" He handed me an open bottle of beer.

"Oh, that you're quite the ladies man—"

"I can't help that." He clinked my bottle with his. "Cheers."

"And that you drop girls like a hot potato if they don't sleep with you."

He pretended to choke on his beer. "Gee, Lynn, don't hold back. Tell me what they're really saying."

"I just did. What time is this movie supposed to start?" I stared straight ahead at the screen pretending to be interested. What I'd told him had surprised me also and now I had to act nonchalant.

"Well, is that what you think of me?" He stared at me until I turned my face to his. Now I clinked his bottle and said, "I don't listen to gossip," which of course wasn't true.

I don't remember what movie we saw that night, some goofy comedy. We got lots of feedback from the speaker and at one point Billy just turned it off. "It's better this way. Let's guess what they're saying." We did that for a while, pretending the actors were portraying high level espionage agents who spoke in deeply serious, staccato tones, saying things like, "My pants are so tight I cannot breathe," and "We will sell you the secrets for three packs of Rolling Rock and a goat."

Billy drank four beers and I drank two. That was enough for me to feel happy and silly, laughing too hard at his jokes. While we kissed, he kept talking like a spy, murmuring in a monotone, "I think my tongue has located your ear and must infiltrate."

My secret. That night in the car I matched my hunger with his face, his body, his scent, which seemed a mixture of pizza and Ivory soap. We didn't sleep together but I knew it wouldn't be long. He knew it too and I became his girlfriend. He didn't dump me and move on to another girl because I was ready to give him what he wanted. I winced only that first time, when he entered me too fast. After that, my body moved with his until my pleasure was so enormous it overtook me, spilling out of my skin and into the night. It made me think of the summer when I was twelve and there was so much rain the reservoir overflowed and flooded the adjoining arboretum.

Carolanne and my girlfriends coyly asked, "*What* are you doing with him?" I was evasive: "Oh, going to the movies, playing miniature golf, riding our bikes." And that much was true. I had no intention of telling them that we were skinny dip-ping at night in the reservoir, running naked through the arboretum until we had no breath left, finally laying down to look up at the stars and twist our limbs together.

But they knew, everyone knew. All you had to do was look at me and Billy to know that our blood pulsed to the same beat, that there was this growing frenzy between us that bordered on something wild.

How long could something like that have lasted? Surely, it would have burnt out, run its course with the summer. But we never got to find out. Billy's mother missed him, want-ed to give him another chance. During the second week of August, he went back to Tulsa. I got a few postcards, a promise to visit often, but by late October there was no pretense of anything.

In the center of my chest was a heavy emptiness. I wasn't able to draw a deep breath because of that weight lodged behind my sternum. It pressed upon me all night as I lay in bed, keeping me awake hour after hour, the clock in the living room chiming away the night.

My esophagus atrophied. I couldn't eat. Chewing and swallowing were too much work so I just drank liquids. When I fainted during our high school's Christmas assembly program, sliding off the wooden folding chair onto the girl next to me, the school nurse sent me home.

My mother screamed the first time she saw me in the doctor's office, my ribs straining against my skin, my limbs so narrow and weak. She had no idea that I'd been starving. For days she would look at me and burst into tears.

During the holidays, I stayed in bed. I drank broth and started to eat scrambled eggs. By mid-January I felt a little better and went back to school. I had so much work to make up and was worried for a time that I wouldn't be able to graduate with my class. I tried to concentrate, to memorize history dates and math formulas. The distraction helped. There were still times when I had to run into the ladies room, hide in a stall and cry as softly as possible, but I was getting better. At lunch time, I sat with my friends in the cafeteria and listened more than talked. Carolanne tried to draw me into the conversation and occasionally I would even laugh. Things were improving. I could eat half a peanut butter and jelly sandwich.

In May, the senior class was preparing for the prom, Banfield's version of The Miss America Pageant. The hair salons put glossy pictures clipped from magazines in the windows and hung signs that said, "Come in for your free prom consultation!" Girls spent days trying on dresses at the local shops or going to fittings at some of the local seamstresses. The adults, most of whom had grown up in town themselves, had prom fever as well. Who was going with whom was discussed at the diner, at the car garage, at the public library. The newspaper did a special issue with prom pictures from the last thirty-five years. My mother has a whole prom scrapbook with black and white snapshots of her and my father standing under an arch of flowers made out of Kleenex.

I had no desire to go, but Carolanne insisted we double-date. Randy Norton, my chemistry lab partner junior year, asked me to be his date and I said okay. Carolanne had been the lead in the spring musical that year, "My Fair Lady." She had always been popular, but now she had a little entourage that followed her around school. She was a shoe-in for prom queen and every guy on the football team asked her to be his date. I was at my locker putting my books away when she told me her choice: Hank Attelby.

"*Him?*" I blurted. "You're going to the prom with *him?*"

My reaction caught her off guard. "Sure, why not him? I thought you liked Hank. I mean he's Billy's cousin…. Oh, is that why?"

Leaning forward, I hid my head in my locker. It was starting, that tremulous feeling in my chest. I swallowed and counted to three. Slowly I realized that it wasn't Hank's relation to Billy that bothered me. No, it was something else. Hank had been nothing until Billy came to town and brought him into focus. After Billy left, my life plummeted; it was a struggle making it through the day. But Hank kept his status. Billy got him into the right crowd and he was still in. This struck me now as terribly unjust.

I emerged from my locker and said as offhandedly as I could, "I'm sorry. It's just that I've always thought of Hank as such a loser. Ever since we were kids and he cried if you said 'boo' to him."

Carolanne rolled her eyes. "That was a long time ago."

"I know. You're right." I pushed my locker shut. "But he was nobody until Billy came to town, and he was only hanging out with us because of Billy. I mean, you have your pick of guys. Why him?"

She looked at me and hesitated a few times before she shrugged and said, "I don't know. I always thought he was cute." She glanced away. "He's got that wavy hair."

Nodding, I said, "Well, if you like him, great. I'm not trying to talk you out of it."

But two days later, it was all over school that Carolanne had told Hank that she wasn't going to the prom with him after all. She hadn't handled it well, telling him that she'd forgotten she'd already accepted an invitation from Jim Sommers, a half-back on the football team.

By that time, everyone was paired up for the prom. Hank had gone from having one of the most sought after dates to not being able to find someone to go with. His status nose-dived when he asked a sophomore, a girl who wore a ridiculous amount of make-up. At the prom, Hank seemed embarrassed by his date and didn't sit with us. Among ourselves, we made plans for graduation parties that didn't include him. Occasionally, I glanced across the gym at Hank, watching him as he handed his date a glass of punch. He seemed mesmerized by Carolanne when she took her walk around the gym wearing her prom queen crown and carrying a spangly scepter. Jim Sommers, a big goofy grin on his face as he escorted her, looked like he couldn't believe his luck. Later my eyes traveled back to Hank's table but he and his date had left early.

I was tired after the round of graduation parties and spent some lazy days sunbathing in the back yard. My mother had already started her regular summer job at the public library and my brother still had two weeks of school before his vacation began. I relished being home alone. The June sun was strong in the open blue sky, the heat slipping through my skin to my bones. I was starting to feel again, to feel something other than empti-ness. The heat was so relentless, so inescapably real.

But one afternoon, after waking from a brief nap on the lawn chair, I sensed my loss as if it were fresh. My eyes were still sealed with sleep, but they were starting to loosen with the moisture of my tears. I had a dreamy sense that I wasn't alone, that Billy was coming between me and the sun, a long shadow interrupting the heat. Gently, I placed my forefinger on my breast and slowly circled the nipple, desire rising in me like sweet dough.

"You slut."

My eyes opened before I realized it. Someone was blocking the sun. Hank. When our eyes met, he frowned and said, "You cheap slut."

My body lurched up the reclining chair. "Get out of here! What do you think you're doing, sneaking up on me like that!"

He stepped forward and swung, his palm striking my face with such force I knew my cheek was stained with an imprint of his hand. Stunned, I held my face and spit at him, my saliva hitting his t-shirt. "You goddamn nobody, get out of here!" I screamed.

Looking at his shirt with disgust, he shook his head as if in disbelief. "You bitch. You fucking bitch." His voice was low and calm, too calm. The soft hairs on my arm stood, sensing

106

menace. A growing ball of ice seemed lodged in my stomach, swelling up towards my throat, choking me.

I swung my feet to the side of the chair and estimated how many steps it would take to get in the house. Would I have time to slam the door and lock it? I tried to stand.

Yank! He pulled my ponytail over my head and made my face swing. "You are such a stupid shit, you know that Lynn Dundee? You are a stupid slut, that's what you are." The voice a hoarse whisper now, his mouth stretched so I noticed the points on his eye teeth. Saliva was pooling in the corners of his lips.

He was pulling my hair so tightly, my scalp ached down to my eyes. "My mother's home," I whispered. I tried to turn my head and bite his arm.

Dropping my ponytail, he laughed, "You lying whore!" With both hands on my shoulders he knocked me back on the lounge chair. He grabbed my bare feet with his hands, his nails slicing their soft undersides. I tried to kick him, but he bit down on my toes and I felt blood snaking over my feet. Shoes! my mind screamed. I need shoes to kick him away! With one jerk, he pulled me down so I was laying flat.

At first, when he was on top of me, my mind left, escaped. Nothing seemed real, even the weight of his body was a trick of some dream. The buzzing rattle of the cicadas was an odd musical accompaniment. Or maybe I was hearing a distant lawnmower. Gradually, I heard him growling into my ear, "Do you think he *loved* you? He couldn't care less about you! He called you 'THE EASY BITCH,' you know that? That's what he called you."

I thought I heard another sound, the opening and closing of a mailbox next door perhaps. Hank heard it too and jumped from me, zipping up his jeans in a single moment. Before he left the yard, he kicked my chair and said, "Billy's marrying his girlfriend in Tulsa. She's knocked up."

I don't know how long it will take me to get better this time. No one knows what I'm going through and that's how I want it. All the books say time and distance can heal anything. There's nothing I can do about time; it has to pass by one day at a time, but I can put so many miles between me and Hank Attelby that someday I won't even remember his name.

I do think about Billy. I can't let myself think too much about what Hank said, if he was lying about things Billy said about me. If I start, my mind gets in a loop and everything around me becomes unreal and I feel like I've lost my balance.

I still walk through the arboretum. It's a lusher shade of green with each passing day. There's so much brush that needs to be cleared away that parts of it are like a jungle. Sometimes I stop and sit on the little bench where Billy and I used to kiss. I take a bite of a doughnut, pleased with how it fills my mouth, how the cinnamon stings my tongue. But then the taste is gone and everything seems artificial again. I have to hurry and take another bite to remind myself that I'm still here.

Leslie Elise Keysor

The Man Who Loved You

for Julia Pastrana

He never looked you in the eyes, but you were used to that. You'd learned as a little girl to look down at your feet so you wouldn't have to see the moment when the expressions twisted from shock into horror, the way the hands flew up to stifle the gasps, to mask the gaping mouths. It never, ever stopped hurting, the way they looked at you. When he lifted the veil from your face, you met the gaze of the crowd with a small, practiced smile, careful to show only a glint of teeth. You couldn't forget how he'd said you looked like a monster when you smiled too broadly—he meant this as a compliment, counting the money he'd collected in the tin box that day, but it made tears rise to the edges of your eyes. *Monster* was one of the only words you understood in English.

His name was Lent. How he'd found you in the tiny village where you were born, you never knew. You were a servant to a family whose children hit you with sticks as you swept the tiled floors and baked loaves of dark bread. You had no family of your own. In exchange for a handful of coins, he took you and two chickens back to America. The chickens died on the train. You sat by the window shivering in your thin dress until he bought you a coat, blue wool with a fox collar. When you put it on, he smiled. You fingered the collar nervously, waiting for the laughter. It was the first time anyone had ever smiled at you without pointing.

Whenever you were scared, you prayed to Mary. There was a small painting near the fireplace in the hallway of the family's home where you used to kneel at night, once the chores were done. You were careful not to let anyone see you. In the painting, Mary held baby Jesus in her arms while all the animals in the stable looked on, full of wonder. You liked the way Mary cradled her son, her lips pressed softly to his forehead. You thought it might be a sin, but sometimes when you cried, you pretended that Mary was holding you. You wondered what that felt like, the comfort of it.

Keysor

Your days were always the same, just in a different town. Through the tent flap, the crowd scuffed the sawdust ground, breathing low, their eyes searching the darkness for the smaller darkness of your face. You stood at the back of the stage, listening for the music to start. Slowly, you began to dance, moving forward in the half-light, bracing yourself. Sometimes you would sing a Spanish song, your voice sweet and sad and surprisingly strong. When you sang, a hush came over the crowd. You became, for a moment, almost human.

The posters of you were grotesque. You avoided them like mirrors, though it was harder. The posters were everywhere. On them, your face was something out of a child's nightmare, your black eyes bulging beneath a low brow, your entire body covered in fur so that no skin was showing. The artist who drew the posters had exaggerated your features: your huge mouth was set in a menacing snarl, your raised hands clawed up like the paws of an animal, ready to attack. In truth your hands were small and gentle, like a little girl's. You could almost imagine they were pretty sometimes, if you turned them at a certain angle. You were billed as "The World's Ugliest Woman!" and though you could not read the words printed beneath your name, they would not have surprised you.

Sometimes there were children in the audience. You felt like you couldn't breathe, looking at them. The little girls in their frilly dresses would cower against their fathers, their eyes sick with fear that whatever had happened to you could somehow happen to them. You watched as they ran their hands across their cheeks, searching each feature in hopes of finding their faces unchanged, the relief that came of not being like you. The boys who stood in front of you were unusually cruel, especially the older ones. They would shout at you, spit in your hair. You knew better than to shield your face. People paid good money to look at you.

You saved the penny he gave you each week to buy cookies, though you never ate them yourself. You gave them to Myra and Lily, who danced on the stage before you. They were timid and mute, women in years only, their dark hair shaved close so that their small skulls appeared pointed. They cried anytime someone raised a voice or laughed in front of them, which was often. On Saturdays, you wrapped four cookies in your handkerchief and waited for them backstage. You taught Myra to reach her hand out in a gesture that meant "more" before you took a second cookie out of your pocket. While they ate, you used the edge of your handkerchief to wipe the tears from one trembling face, then the other.

Lent owned you, but he did little things for you that were kind. He stroked your hair when you were falling asleep on the train. He taught you to recite "The Lord's Prayer" in English. He'd filled your bathrobe pockets with candy once when he found you crying backstage, the sobs rising in your throat so that speech was impossible. You started sneaking glances of him when you were certain he wasn't looking. The sight of him gave you a strange, sick feeling in your stomach. In the rare moments when you were alone, you danced around the hotel room in his favorite red dress, repeating his name softly to yourself, like a mantra.

If you knew the marriage was a publicity stunt, you never let on. You stood together in front of the minister, your face shrouded in a heavy veil, listening to the words, *love, honor, cherish.* He did not hold your hand. When it was time to kiss you, his lips brushed the air. Your eyes were bright and naïve as you told one of the witnesses, another manager from the sideshow, what you believed to be true: *He loves me for my own sake.*

He did not want you to touch him. You had to lie on your hands sometimes, because otherwise you kept reaching for him. You waited for him to roll off you, the steady breathing of his sleep, before you allowed yourself to cry quietly into the scarf that covered your face.

There were other women, of course. He made you sing for them while they sat in his lap, drinking wine. Sometimes he told you to strip and you did, your small hands fumbling with the buttons at the back of your dress. You felt the blood drum under your cheeks when you turned to face them.

You had only one prayer when you found out you were pregnant: that the baby would look like him. You imagined a child with the same delicate nose, the same sparse golden hair. Your prayer was not answered. The baby was tiny and mis-shapen, covered in downy black hair. He lived for thirty-six hours without ever opening his eyes. After he stopped breathing, you wouldn't let go of him. The midwife waited silently by your bed, looking down at the floor. Your cries were fierce and guttural, like an injured animal.

You died within the week.

Keysor

Your husband paced the hospital room, beating the wall with his fist until it bled. He was out of work. An undertaker wanted to buy the bodies and Lent sold them to him for the price of a month's ticket sales. When your husband saw you three days later, he almost expected to see you break into a shy smile. The mummification was startling. He quickly paid twice as much as he'd earned so that he could get the bodies back. He arranged for a special glass case to be built for you and his son. The baby wore a velvet suit and stood clipped to a perch, like a bird. You were dressed in an embroidered red dress with ribbons woven through your hair. Standing with your hands on your hips, you appeared, for the first time, unashamed. You could no longer sing or dance, but people still lined up to see you. You were unable to look away.

Your husband died in an asylum twenty years later. He had terrible hallucinations. Monsters danced in and out of his dreams, singing Spanish songs. He repeatedly clawed at his face in front of the mirror, trying to find a face that did not scare him. He would not fall asleep in a room unless the lights were on.

Your story does not end here.

You traveled from town to town with your son, from owner to owner. The crowds kept coming. They stood in front of you, their expressions registering pity and disbelief. Staring back at them, your glass eyes were unforgiving. You continued to search the faces in the crowd for more than a hundred years, looking for the man who loved you.

Judith Arcana

SHEILA'S DEPOSITION, 1997

    Ok, look, don't give me a hard time; I'm gonna tell every-
thing; it doesn't matter now anyway. I need a cigarette....
Alright. Here goes. In my own words, like you like to say. First
of all, I never thought I'd get, you know, pregnant, because I
just didn't, you know, I mean it was too stupid, I mean, like
who gets pregnant? I figured nobody gets pregnant, really. And
it's not like we did it that many times either. And then when it
happened, it took a while before I even knew, because I wasn't
always bleeding at the same time every month, I wasn't some
poster girl who started every twenty-eight days like they say, so
I didn't even notice at first. And I didn't want to pay any attention anyway, it's so gross, I mean, the whole thing. Like blood
always gets on your hands when you change and half the time
it starts when you're at school and you don't even know 'til you
pull down your pants in the locker room. But when I started to
get fat I got freaked out; that's when I remembered I hadn't
seen my period for a while. So I went on really strict diets,
almost like the anorexic girls, and I worked out as many hours
as I could, and that really helped, so like nobody noticed. My
father never looks at me anyway, he wouldn't recognize me on
the street, I swear, and my mother is not in the picture, you
know? Later, when my stomach started to stick out anyway, I
just wore really long sweaters and shirts, dark, mostly black.
When I was naked you could really tell; I showed Jerry in the
seventh month and he said, Jeez, how much bigger is it gonna
get? But I had this cool idea, I went and got—really, you won't
believe this, I got a *girdle,* you know, like women used to wear
in old times. I got it in the old lady section of a store downtown
where nobody goes, and it worked, you know, like even when I
was eight months and all the way to the end, nobody noticed
anything—well nobody ever said they did, anyway. It hurt
though, I mean that girdle really hurt me. And when it finally
started to come out, when I felt it hurting *under* the girdle, like
from the inside, I was in school, so I got Jerry and we skipped
out in his car. First we just drove around, but then he took me

113

to a motel we used for sex, and I stayed in the bathroom until it came out. He played music real loud so nobody could hear me—I mean, I wasn't like some jungle woman or anything, but I made noise. When it came out, I turned it over and we pressed the head into a pile of towels for a while. We filled the tub with water to clean up and first we just put it all in there, the rest of the stuff that came out, you know, like the afterbirth, the cord. Jerry cut the cord with a Swiss army knife—he was very together. He used to be some kind of scout—you know, they learn stuff. We watched it float for a while, and then Jerry said, Hey, I know what we can do; let's take it to a dumpster—'cause who looks in dumpsters, right? I mean, nobody we know does that, only maybe, like, homeless people, they might look around in there, but they're not gonna care. I mean, ok, they eat from dumpsters, but they're not gonna eat a baby, right? And it'd be dead anyway, and we can like stick it in a box, or under news-papers; nobody's ever gonna see it. So, ok, we were wrong about that part, but we did a pretty good job. You can't tell me it'd be better if we got all nice and married and kept the kid, playing Mommy and Daddy. I mean, think about it.

PMS

Noreen's Phone Calls, 1999

They told me everything the day I left the hospital; they spread the papers out in front of me and I signed, but I never read them. I pretty much knew what they said. They explained the rules, about how I would never see her again, how I would never know who got her. Just like when it happened, I did what I was told. See, I was never a complainer; I was the kind that even if I fell down and hurt myself, I'd get right back up and keep walking. He lived on my block, we went out a few times; he seemed ok. We went to a movie and had ice cream after, but when we cut through the alley on the way home, he pushed me up against the back of a building. I saw him a lot on the street after that but I never talked to him. And I never told what happened, even when I knew I was pregnant. I dropped out of school and moved into the Home when it started to show. We sang hymns after supper every night, played cards every afternoon; we did a lot of laundry. They advised us to give them away; there wasn't much talk about taking care of babies. They always said the babies would be better off with their new parents; their new parents would give them good homes, send them to college. Once I was out of there, I hardly ever thought about it. That's the truth. I didn't cry when I saw babies, or wonder what she looked like; it was gone from me, like she was gone from me. It was erased, wiped out of my mind for years. Then one day I saw in the newspaper about some people who were adopted searching for their birth mothers. I'd never heard the expression before—*birth mother*. I started to cry. Picture this, I'm on the train, I don't have any Kleenex or anything, and I can't stop crying. I mean, *sobbing*. I got off before my stop, I was so embarrassed. Two days later, like I was hypnotized, I picked up the phone book, found the agency that handled the adoption, and called. While I was picking out the numbers on the phone pad, my head started buzzing—literally buzzing; I could hear this buzz behind my eyes. It stopped the second they answered. The second they picked up the phone, there was a clear silence, like a sheet of window glass, clear silence hanging in my head where the buzzing had been. Then the person on

115

the other end said *Hello. Hello?* and I started to talk. I told them if she ever came looking, I wanted to be found. I gave them my home number and address, my number and address at the gallery, my email and cell phone—I would have given driving directions, the buses and trains that stop near me, or my social security number and my blood type—but they already had that. I didn't search on my own, hire a detective like some do. I only wanted to make myself available; in case she ever wanted to know, she could find me. And what they did was, they sent her a letter, saying if she wanted to meet her birth mother, they had the information. I didn't know it could work that way, but that's what happened. After a long time (she thought about it nearly a year) she called me. And when the phone rang—I swear to god this is true—when the phone rang, I knew before I picked it up that it was her.

TAIL

I woke up because something was pressing against me, a hard knot in my lower back. I rolled over and felt the bed, the sheets, the quilt. Nothing. It made me think of camping, the roots and stones under the sleeping bag. I stood up and ran my arm in sweeping motions over the mattress. Nothing. Sun poured across the bed.

Even as I bent to check the mattress, I could feel whatever it was still pressing against me, in the same spot. Slowly, I reached around, hiked up my nightgown and put my hand on my back.

There was a lump under my skin. Hard, bony, unmovable. I carried a chair into the bathroom and stood on it. I turned and lifted my nightgown, and there, perfectly centered above the crack of my ass, was the lump. Sideways it looked like a little tent, as though someone were pushing a drumstick through from the other side. I stood there and stared. My pale bottom and thighs, the strange thing on my back.

I got down and put the chair back in the kitchen. I stood and looked out the window. There was a cold hard sunlight on the morning. The neighbor boy slammed out of his door and ran down the weedy driveway between my rental house and his. I watched him, his thin legs beneath him, and I thought, *Cancer.*

Cancer. I put my fingers in my mouth, four of them, and bit down. Impossible! I was alive and whole! I thought about crying, or calling my mother or brother but I didn't do those things. Just stood there, vaguely wishing there was coffee, and then I made some. Maybe I shouldn't have made coffee if I was dying of cancer but what the hell else would I do on a Sunday morning? I couldn't go to the doctor's office. And nobody went to the emergency room for lumps, did they? What was done with lumps anyhow? Removed, dissolved? Did they usually appear overnight?

I watered the plants. I read the comics and watched a movie. Sometimes whole blocks of hours went by and I forgot about the lump, and when I remembered it, I wasn't as frightened as I should have been. It was backwards. I felt as though there was something wrong with me because I wasn't frightened, not because I had the growth on my back.

It was like I'd been waiting for it.

By Monday morning it had grown into a stub. Longer, thicker, more prominent. I called off work and made an appointment with a doctor. I didn't really want to go.

I sat in the cold office wearing a pale blue gown. I didn't like the doctor who came in the room. He smelled like moth balls. He measured the stub on my back. He wrote "three inch protrusion" on a chart, felt the stub with hard fingers, pressed the skin around it.

He said, "Bone spur."

He sent me in for x-rays. I was face down on a table, covered by that heavy lead blanket that's been touched by everyone in the world and suddenly I thought, *it's not cancer.* I was so sure that I would have gotten up and left right then if it wouldn't have been so impolite.

When the doctor looked at the x-rays, he shook his head. He prescribed anti-inflammatory pills, painkillers, and an anti-calcifying agent. He made an appointment for me with a spine specialist, a friend of his. He spoke as though he wished he were elsewhere, half-looking at me, half-looking at the wall behind me.

Finally I said, "Look, I don't think there's really anything wrong with me."

He laughed scornfully and said, "Of course there's something wrong with you. You're growing something and unless it's a tumor or a baby, you're past the age for growing things." I took the prescription slips and thanked him but I didn't get them filled, and I didn't believe him.

After all, it didn't hurt. It grew.

My suitpants and skirts didn't fit over the stub comfortably so I went to a flea market and bought a pile of those gauzy Indian print skirts, with elastic waists, for five bucks. It was far from corporate dress but nobody ever saw me anyhow. They just breezed past my desk on their important business, nodding at me maybe, or asking for new messages. I could have had a blue face. Come to think of it, we all could have blue faces in that office, for as much as anyone looked at anyone else. But what did I know? Maybe they had parties together, barbeques or luaus. I wouldn't have gone if I'd been invited. I'm no good at small talk.

I started wearing the skirts right away, and no one said
a thing.

Eventually the stub became what it obviously was: a tail.
Pink and fresh skinned, it grew long. Close to my back it was
thick, almost two inches across, but the further it got away from
me, it grew gradually thinner and more flexible, with a nice
round tip at the end, like a pencil eraser.

I called my friend Rhonda in Virginia and she said, "You're
kidding, a tail?"

I said, "I'm not kidding."

She said, "Why on earth would you grow a tail?"

"I don't know."

She said, "Jesus. Can't they surgically remove it or something?"

I said, "That would be amputation! I don't think I want it
removed. I don't."

She said. "Of course you do. Jesus. A tail! You have to have
it removed. It's ridiculous. You can't walk around with a tail.
It's not normal."

"But—," I said.

"But nothing. Is it growing out of your head? Use some
common sense, girl. Who's ever going to marry a girl with
a tail?"

"Rhonda," I said, "don't tell anyone."

"Don't worry," she said, "I wouldn't want to."

I slept on my side or my belly and sometimes I woke up with
my back aching from the effort of not rolling over. One day I
realized I'd been awake for awhile, just staring at the water
spots on my window and I started to cry. Just like that, finally. I
thought: It's not cancer, it's not malignant, it won't kill me. But
it's a tail and it's going to follow me forever and now nobody,
anywhere, will ever really understand. It was going to be me
and this tail alone.

Because of the tail, I avoided chairs with flat hard backs. I
had to think first and shut doors slowly after I passed through
them. In the shower I ran the length of the tail with a soapy
washcloth, just as if it had always been there, needing to
be washed.

After a couple of weeks the tail became bristly. Then the
bristles grew longer. At first there was a nice coat of short fur,
and then that coat grew. The fur was gray, a dove colored gray,

with occasional stripes of white. I couldn't say they were even full stripes. Maybe more like streaks. It was healthy looking fur, long and soft.

The tail hung from above my ass, sort of pulling on the skin of my back. I didn't mind. It felt sexy to have it bobbing there, moving in time with my hips. Sexy in a way I'd never been. Sexy like movie stars or naturally beautiful women, a sexiness I couldn't help. I didn't try to move the tail on my own, but once or twice when I was sitting down to eat, I saw the tip come into sight and then whip away. I pretended not to notice. How could it move without me?

It followed me around the apartment, swishing out from beneath my skirt or nightie as I walked. It dragged on the floor and slammed into doorjambs if I turned the corner too fast. This didn't hurt so much but it was uncomfortable. Those knocks thumped all the way up my spine. When my spine was thumped like that, from a really good whack, my head buzzed for an hour afterwards.

The tail cleaned the floors of my house like a dust mop. Furls of dust and hair, bits of plastic and string and lint and fingernail clippings. Soon it needed grooming. I bought a nice hairbrush with a wooden back and rounded bristles. I combed the fur until it was clean again, shiny and without mats.

When I went out, I looped the tail up under my skirt with a wide piece of burgundy colored ribbon.

Still, it was a problem at work. I couldn't sit comfortably in my office chair any more. I leaned forward all day, my back knotted and stiff.

Sometimes the tail slipped free from the ribbon after I sat too long. One day on my way to the copier I passed Jean Tertlebaum's desk and I felt it come loose. It fell on the floor behind me with a whump. Jean looked up and I kept going. The next day she leaned over my counter and asked me conspiratorially if I'd brought my dog to work. I told her I didn't have a dog. She looked at me, irritated. She said, "You ought to know by now who to trust around here."

I did know who to trust around there and that was nobody. I didn't trust her, not one bit, but I wasn't going to lie, either. Later I thought it was stupid of me not to just show her. The tail just showed up, after all, it's not something shameful that I went out and bought, or a habit I ought to hide. Why should she have cared? But then I thought of Rhonda, and how she hadn't called since I told her about the tail, and I was glad I'd kept my mouth shut.

All day, five days a week, I took phone calls for the brokers in their hive of offices. I directed their calls down the halls and corridors. I buzzed people in and out. I took messages, I took calls, took rudeness. Suddenly, I was bored with it. I no longer dreamt that someone would notice how efficient I was, that someone might call one day to find out about that pleasant and useful woman at the front desk. I realized how silly it was to think that anyone would ever call down and say that.

I saved my tail grooming for work. I brought my brush with me. The fur was quite thick by now. I picked things out of it and put them in a small pile on my desk next to my pink message pad. I combed the longest parts of the fur and made them pliable. Some days, with a little spit, I wrapped lengths of fur around my index finger to make curls. It took such a long time to clean the tail thoroughly, that the time at work passed much more quickly.

I didn't always feel like answering the phone anymore. I began missing calls.

When I did answer the phone, I spoke the name of the firm, waited until they said who they wanted (never me, why would they want me? I didn't want them either) and sent them on through. Often, all the little lights lit up at once and I didn't hurry. I went through one by one. They could wait or hang up. I didn't care.

One day, at the rush time for phone calls, I'd left my tail curled on the desk in front of me while I took care of the lines. There was a tricky knot in it that I was picking loose with a paperclip.

It was a moment before I realized Mr. Lee, the boss, was in front of my desk staring down at my tail, which almost entirely obscured the desk calendar blotter. His cologne was so strong I coughed.

He said incredulously, "Is that an animal you've brought to work, Miss?"

I said, "This is *my tail*." It was the first time I'd said it aloud and I could feel the blush all over my face.

He lifted his upper lip in displeasure and said, "Don't joke with me. Animals are not permitted at work. This is a place of business."

"You don't understand," I said. "This is my tail." I stared at his blotchy cheeks and nose. I realized I hated him. Not only him, but myself when I was there. Hated the place, hated the phones, hated the urgency everyone pretended was real.

I stood up and let the tail slide off the desk on its own. It swung out behind me, rustling out to the back of my skirt. I gathered the few things that belonged to me there at my desk: a miniature African violet, my purse, a couple of pens.

"This is a stupid job," I said to him as I passed, surprising myself.

I walked across the floor to the elevator, pressed the down button and felt my tail swishing behind me like an angry cat's. I could feel him staring at me. Jerk, jerk, jerk! I thought. That's when it happened. My tail lifted all by itself and whapped hard on the ground, once, twice, three times. The elevator door opened and I got on. I turned and in a single motion, lifted my tail like a train on a gown, and pulled it in after me. Elegant tail!

I stopped wearing it doubled up under my skirt. I wore it free, hanging or flapping or dragging behind me everywhere I went. In the grocery store, at the bank, around the neighborhood. I worked at learning to lift it and move it on its own but it wasn't like arms or legs. It seemed to have its own sense of momentum, or maybe it was too new. Anyhow, I didn't have much control over it.

People thought it was a costume tail. Sometimes they mentioned it while I checked out with my groceries. Asked me if I was in a play, asked me if I was going to a party. I told them, it's my tail. One time a woman with two children and a grocery cart full of toilet paper and frozen tater tots stared hard at me and the tail and then moved her kids and cart into another line. It embarrassed me, that she would react like that, as if I were contagious or beastly or wrong. I didn't know what to do. I stood there and stared at the magazines on the rack in front of me and suddenly I felt the tail swinging behind me, high and indignant.

I called my mother in Florida and told her, "I've grown a tail." She didn't take it so well, but I tried to explain. "I can't help it, Mom. Yes, I went to the doctor. No, he can't do anything. No, he can't."

My brother Michael called to confirm the news. I told him, "Yes, it's true." I said, "Do you know what? It's kind of pretty. Really. It's not all bad."

He said, "No? Well, I goddamn better not grow one. I'm telling you right now." Then he hung up on me.

My mother called back a week later and said, "Having a tail, darling, is not as glamorous as you might think."

I said, "I know that, Mom."

At night I wrapped the tail around me. Sleeping on my side I curled it up and over me. I dug my fingers into the loose knots of it and slept like that, holding it. Or it holding me. There were days that I thought my tail was the most beautiful thing I'd ever seen. That it was more beautiful, by far, than the rest of me. Days like these, the tail was everything. It seemed a force of its own, beyond me. It grew out of me, it used my body to travel, but somehow its beauty was aside from me, or maybe merely including me. I couldn't decide if I should take credit for it. But it did belong to me, and if it did belong to me, then did that I mean that I was beautiful, that I was somehow special? After all the years of unremarkable living, did it mean that I'd become remarkable?

But there were other days, bad days, when I barely lifted it over doorsteps and puddles. I dragged it because it was heavy, because it was what made me different from everyone. Those days I thought that it only made me uglier than I'd already been.

People in the neighborhood began noticing more often. I heard them whispering after I'd passed. They no longer spoke directly to me, only about me. It made me feel bad.

One day my landlord, who lives in the building next door, called out to me as I went by. He was painting the wrought iron railing on the outside stair of his building.

He said, "That ain't no costume tail, now is it."

I stopped and said, "No, no, it certainly isn't."

He took a big breath, puffing out his belly, and said, "A tail. That's sure interesting. Now I may just be an old-fashioned guy, but I don't know. I'm not sure it's right for people to go around flashing their tails as if they're something to be proud of."

I said, "I don't know that many people who have tails at all, Mr. Whitsun, or I'd have a better formed idea of how they carry themselves with them."

He frowned at me and I stared right back at him until he turned and began painting and then I went on.

This kind of conversation made me nervous. It was getting to be time for me to work again, I was beginning to need the money, and there's Mr. Whitsun acting as if there's some code of behavior around tails. Things were looking bad.

I watched people walk, two-legged, non-tailed people. They strolled through the park, jumped over curbs. They ran after their dogs, light, upright, clean moving on their two legs. Nothing snagged behind them on tree roots or caught on grates. Sometimes I got jealous. I thought, they make living look so easy.

After a while the tail got so thick and wide, it was almost as heavy as me. In the center, it was wide like a beaver's tail. I could barely lift it. It dragged everywhere. Mud caked and hardened into a crust along the bottom of it. It took all my body's strength leaning against it to get it to move. Worse, it began to smell. It hung outside my bed, too heavy to curl up over me anymore. I felt sorry every time I looked at it.

There was a laundromat around the corner from my apartment with benches out front. I began spending my days on the benches (it took almost thirty minutes to drag my tail down there) and I filled my time watching people go by. This made me feel worse. The people in my neighborhood wore faces that were bent and pulled and knotted like old ropes. They argued with each other and frowned over the weather. I didn't want to be like them, living their lives, but I didn't want to be like me either.

Then one night I dreamt that my tail fell off. I was walking up a steep staircase and suddenly, it dropped away from me. I almost fell forward from being so light. It slid away, down the staircase without me, and I felt it leave. A hole grew inside me like a tomb.

The next night I dreamt that I was sitting in a chair, interviewing for a job, when the tail fell right away from me and hit the floor with a big dead thump. I said to the lady who was interviewing me, "I'll have to bury that," and as soon as I said it I began to cry.

I woke up from these dreams sweating and frightened. I didn't know what any of it meant.

My mother called. She said, "Still have the tail, Miss Mouse?"

"No, Mom," I said, "I took it off and hung it up in the closet. You can borrow it for Halloween."

She was silent on the other end of the phone and then she said, "You have no idea how hard this is for me."

I dreamt the tail was on a long kitchen table behind me. It was stretched out the length of the table and I was alone, waiting. A man in a donkey mask came in the room. He spoke to me but the mask garbled his words. He took a knife off the counter behind him and before I could speak he chopped my tail off. Blood poured out of me and out of the stump on the table. I was screaming.

I woke up frantic. I put both hands to my tail. It was there, hanging to the floor beside me. I felt terrible then, terrible that I hadn't been combing it or cleaning it or even treating it like it belonged to me. Poor old tail, stinking like that in the first light of morning.

I got out of bed and dragged it to the bathroom. Sun was streaming in the window over the tub and it caught the sprinkles of water as the tub filled, making little hair-like splashes of light. I heaved my tail over the edge of the tub and felt the water filling up around it. The water turned brown and muddy right away, so I filled the tub and emptied it a couple of times before I even got out the shampoo. But when it was time, and the water was reasonably clean, I started working on that tail, starting at the tip and working all the way up to my ass, I scrubbed and scrubbed and dug my fingernails in and scratched out all that was lodged and wedged and matted. The end of the tail, once it was clean, even began to float down at the end of the tub.

Once I'd finished scrubbing every inch of it, I rinsed it twice, put in some de-tangler and rinsed it again. I used three towels to dry it and then walked out to the balcony of my apartment. The sun was shining full out there and I sat down on the deck, leaning against the building behind me. I pulled the tail into my lap, where it lay drying. I thought about how it would be fluffy and full when it was done. I absentmindedly petted it while I sat there. After a while I dozed off.

When I woke, I found my tail had dried, and not only that, it had curled itself up my body and around my shoulders. I leaned into it, running the fur through my fingers, and wondered who would hire a woman with a tail that she refused to hide.

Judith Arcana's writing has appeared most recently in collections from *Calyx Press, Chicory Blue Press,* and *Witness.* She is the author of *Grace Paley's Life Stories: A Literary Biography* and a collection of poetry, "Maternal Instinct," for which she is seeking a publisher. She lives in Portland, Oregon and is a member of the doctoral faculty of The Union Institute.

Halsted Mencotti Bernard lives, works, and writes in the San Francisco Bay Area. She discovered the Bay Area during the start-up boom of the late 90s and, like most people who did, no longer works for a start-up. She currently presides over the circulation of a small university library and writes poetry when the books let her rest.

Wendy L. Burk lives in Arizona. With collaborative poet Eric Magrane, she has served as Artist-in-Residence at Isle Royale National Park and Buffalo National River. She is a translator of Spanish and English for literature, schools, and non-profit organizations.

Heather Burmeister's work has appeared in *The Sulphur River Literary Review, Blue Collar Review,* and *BadNewsBingo.* A baker and line cook, she volunteers for Write Around Portland, takes evening classes, and hopes to one day teach and own her own home.

Karla Clark lives and works in Northern California. In 1998, she won the Anna Davidson Rosenberg prize in the category of "Emerging Poet." Her poems have appeared in *convulvulus, Pi Kappa Phi Forum,* and *Runes,* and she is the author of the chapbook, *What Made Moon.*

Trish Steinley Davis, a mixed-blood Cherokee born in Poteau, Oklahoma, now lives in the Hudson Valley outside of New York City. She has an MA in literature, has taught writing, and has poetry forthcoming in the anthology, *The Kitchen Table Diaries.*

Denise Duhamel's most recent books are *Queen for a Day: Selected and New Poems* (University of Pittsburgh Press, 2001) and *Sweet Jesus: Poems about the Ultimate Icon* (The Anthology Press, 2002), which she co-edited with Nick Carbó. She teaches creative writing at Florida International University in Miama.

Elaine Equi is the author of several books of poetry, most recently *The Cloud of Knowable Things* (Coffee House Press, 2003). Her other books include *Surface Tension, Decoy,* and the winner of the San Francisco State Poetry Award, *Voice-Over.* She teaches in the MFA program at The

New School in New York City and in the graduate program at City College of New York.

Zan Gay spent a rural 1950s childhood in Florida before studying art in Europe and earning degrees in Art History and Library Science. Her poems have appeared or are forthcoming in *Karamu, Paper Street Press, Feminist Studies,* and *Slant.* A resident of Coral Springs, Florida, she currently works as an art museum docent.

Lois Marie Harrod is the author of numerous books of poetry including *Crazy Alice* (Belle Mead Press, 1991), *Spelling the World Backward* (Palanquin Press, 2000), and the most recent chapbook, *Put Your Sorry Side Out* (Concrete Wolf 2003). The winner of a 2003 New Jersey Council on the Arts poetry fellowship, her poems have appeared in many journals including *American Poetry Review, The Carolina Quarterly, PMS,* and *Prairie Schooner.* A Geraldine R. Dodge poet, she currently teaches English at Voorhees High School.

Marianna Hofer runs Blue Room Studio, a writing and photography space in the historic Jones Building in downtown Findlay, Ohio. She teaches English at the University of Findlay.

Mary Kaiser lives in Birmingham, Alabama, with her husband and their two children. Her poems have appeared in *Eclipse* and *Perihelion.*

Leslie Elise Keysor is a Special Education teacher who lives in Birmingham, Alabama, with her husband and one-year-old son. Her short story, "Skeleton Gloves," won first place in *Birmingham Magazine*'s 2000 Summer Fiction contest. Her work has also appeared in *The Dan River Anthology* and *The Richmond Arts Magazine.*

Sandra Kohler's poems have appeared in such magazines as *The New Republic, Prairie Schooner, PMS,* and *5 AM.* Her first book of poems, *The Country of Women,* was published by Calyx Press in 1995 and her second, *The Ceremonies of Longing,* won the 2002 AWP Award Series in Poetry and was published in 2003 by the University of Pittsburgh Press. She lives and writes in Selinsgrove, a small town on the Susquehanna River in central Pennsylvania.

Kerry Langan has published short fiction in a number of literary magazines including *Story Quarterly, Cimarron Review,* and *American Literary Review.* Her novel, "The Theater of Happiness," is seeking a home. She lives and writes in Oberlin, Ohio.

Irene Latham lives in Birmingham, Alabama with her husband and three sons. Her chapbook, *Now Playing,* was published in 2001 and her poems have or will appear in *Flyaway, Birmingham Arts Review, Talking River Review,* and *White Pelican Review.*

Naomi Levine has published poetry or had poetry accepted in such journals as *The Jabberwock Review, Poetry Motel,* and *Raw Dog Press.* An active member of New Jersey Women Who Write, she lives in Parsippany.

Tammara Lindsay's work can be found most recently in *Can We Have Our Ball Back?* She hails from State College, Pennsylvania.

Ada Long is quite simply a queen. A Professor of English at the University of Alabama at Birmingham, she dares to retire this year from her long-esteemed position as Founder and Director of UAB's Honors Program; it celebrates its 21st birthday this year. She and her short-timer cohort, Dail, will soon be happy and hopefully lazy residents of St. George Island off the Gulf Coast of Florida. We are mighty lucky to have her words grace our pages. We will miss her around the farm.

Karen Maceira is a past Ruth Lilly National Collegiate Poetry Convocation participant and her poems have appeared in such publications as *The Beloit Poetry Journal, The New Orleans Review,* and *Negative Capability.* A native of New Orleans with an MFA from Penn State, she now teaches high school in Pearl River, Louisiana.

Janet McCann is the author and co-author of many books and the winner of many awards. A 1989 NEA Creative Writing Fellowship winner, she has taught at Texas A&M University since 1969 and was until recently the coordinator of creative writing there. Her most recent collection is *Looking for Buddha in the Barbed Wire Garden* (Avisson, 1996) and her poems have appeared in such journals as *Kansas Quarterly, Parnassus, Nimrod, New York Quarterly,* and *McCall's.*

Eileen Murphy recently traded Chicago for her hometown of Lakeland, Florida where she now practices law (probate, real estate) part-time in a storefront office. Her poems have appeared in such journals as *The Louisville Review, Mudfish, Poetry Motel, Lonzie's Fried Chicken,* and Sam Hamill's *Poets Against the War.*

Mendi Lewis Obadike lives in Connecticut and teaches at Wesleyan University. Her first book of poetry, *Armor and Flesh,* is forthcoming from Lotus Press. A Cave Canem fellow, she is also the librettist of the opera *The Sour Thunder* (composed with Keith Obadike) which premiered as the first new media art commission from the Yale Cabaret, later to be broadcast internationally from Berlin.

Carla Panciera lives in Rowley, Massachusetts. Her poetry, fiction, and memoirs have appeared in several journals including *The Chattahoochee Review, Nimrod, Kalliope,* and *Under the Sun.*

Nancy Powers is a journalist and an MFA student at the University of Missouri-St. Louis. In addition to winning several local prizes, her work has appeared in *Fan,* and *Small Spiral Notebook,* and is forthcoming in *The Mankato Poetry Review.* A life-long St. Louisan, she is a grandmother and devoted Cardinal fan.

Elizabeth Rollins received a 2003 Prose Fellowship from the New Jersey Council on the Arts. Her work has appeared previously in *Philadelphia's CityPaper, W.C. Magazine, friskmagazine, High Maintenance, The Redwood Coast Review,* and on-line at storyglossia.com.

L.J. Rose jumped off the career ladder in 1993 and undertook a 55,000 mile, 2-year, 29-country, solo journey that circled the globe. Her experiences inspired her to work in Mother Teresa's Home for the Dying. An organizational consultant, coach, and speaker, her home base is now San Francisco.

Kathleen Roxby is a former teacher of English and Drama who now works as a project manager in information technology. She hosts a monthly poetry reading at Borders Bookstore in Goleta, California and her work has appeared in *Art/Life* and *Voce Piena,* as well as the anthologies *Electric Rain* and *Poetry Zone Poets.*

Carly Sachs is a high school English teacher in the Bronx. A native of Ohio, she recently graduated from the MFA program at the New School University in New York City. Her work has appeared or is forthcoming in *Another Chicago Magazine, slope #17, goodfoot, PMS,* and *The Chiron Review.* Her last *PMS* publication, a poem called "the story," won her a spot in *Best American Poetry 2004.*

Sonia Sanchez is an acclaimed poet, dramatist, and civil rights activist. Born in Birmingham and now living in Philadelphia, she is the author of over 16 books of poetry including *We a BaddDDD People* (1970), *Under a Soprano Sky* (1987), and *Shake Loose My Skin: New and Selected Poems* (1999). In 1985, she received the American Book Award for *Homegirls and Handgrenades* (1984), and she has won *The Quarterly Black Review*'s Phyllis Wheatley Award, the Robert A. Frost Award, the Lindback Award for Distinguished Teaching, and the Patricia Lucretia Mott award, all of which acknowledge her contributions to African American literature and activism. She is the 2004 recipient of the Harper Lee Award for Alabama's Distinguished Writer, an event that marks the first time she has been so recognized as a writer of the South.

Mary Eila Smothers is a twenty-two-year-old native of Talladega, Alabama, and a senior at Samford University where she majors in history. She serves with the U.S. Army 214th MP Company in Baghdad as part of the Alabama Army National Guard unit from Alexander City, Alabama. Currently instructing at the Baghdad Policy Academy, she went to Irag on May 27, 2003, and hopes to head back to the United States on May 27, 2004.

Jeanie Thompson has published three collections of poetry including *How To Enter the River, Witness,* and *White for Harvest: New and Selected Poems.* New work is forthcoming in *Louisville Review, Maize,* and *River Styx.* With Jay Lamar, she edited *The Remembered Gate: Memoirs by Alabama Writers.* She is a member of the poetry faculty in Spalding University's Brief Residency MFA Writing Program in Louisville, Kentucky, and founding director of the Alabama Writers' Forum, a partnership program of the Alabama State Council on the Arts.

Lynne Thompson is a native of Los Angeles and a recovering attorney nowing working at UCLA in Human Resources. Her work has been published or will be forthcoming in *The Indiana Review, Louisiana Literature, Pearl, Rattle,* and *Runes.* Her chapbook, *We Arrive by Accumulation,* was published in 2002.

Maria Vargas was born in Managua, Nicaragua and now lives in Birmingham, Alabama. Her book of poetry in Spanish, *Los Ojos Abiertos del Silencio (The Open Eyes of Silence)* was the winner of the Rafaela Contreras Poetry Prize for Central American Women Writers and was published in 2003. The contest, in which women from the six Central American countries participated, is named for the Salvadoran writer and wife of Ruben Dario, a Nicaraguan poet widely acknowledged as the creator of Modernism in Spanish literature.

Holly Welker has published poetry, fiction, and non-fiction in a variety of magazines and journals including *Black Warrior Review, Cumberland Poetry Review, Gulf Coast, Hayden's Ferry Review,* and *PMS.* She has a PhD from the University of Iowa and is an assistant professor of creative writing at Penn State Erie, The Behrend College.

Patti White teaches American literature and creative writing at Ball State University. Winner of a number of awards including the Hopewell Prize for Poetry (1994), first place in the Literal Lattee Food Verse Awards (2000), and the Anhinga Prize for Poetry (2001), her collection of poems, *Tackle Box,* was published by Anhinga Press in 2002.